1 & 2
THESSALONIANS

J. Vernon M

THOMAS NELSON
Since 1798

NASHVILLE   DALLAS   MEXICO CITY   RIO DE JANEIRO

Published in Nashville, Tennessee, by Thomas Nelson, Inc.

Scripture quotations are from the KING JAMES VERSION of the Bible.

Library of Congress Cataloging-in-Publication Data

McGee, J. Vernon (John Vernon), 1904–1988
   [Thru the Bible with J. Vernon McGee]
   Thru the Bible commentary series / J. Vernon McGee.
     p.   cm.
   Reprint. Originally published: Thru the Bible with J. Vernon McGee. 1975.
   Includes bibliographical references.
   ISBN 0-7852-1053-9 (TR)
   ISBN 0-7852-1112-8 (NRM)
   1. Bible—Commentaries. I. Title.
BS491.2.M37 1991
220.7'7—dc20   90–41340
ISBN: 978-0-7852-0797-9   CIP

Printed in the United States

HB 04.16.2024

CONTENTS

1 THESSALONIANS

2 THESSALONIANS

PREFACE

The radio broadcasts of the Thru the Bible Radio five-year program were transcribed, edited, and published first in single-volume paperbacks to accommodate the radio audience.

There has been a minimal amount of further editing for this publication. Therefore, these messages are not the word-for-word recording of the taped messages which went out over the air. The changes were necessary to accommodate a reading audience rather than a listening audience.

These are popular messages, prepared originally for a radio audience. They should not be considered a commentary on the entire Bible in any sense of that term. These messages are devoid of any attempt to present a theological or technical commentary on the Bible. Behind these messages is a great deal of research and study in order to interpret the Bible from a popular rather than from a scholarly (and too-often boring) viewpoint.

We have definitely and deliberately attempted "to put the cookies on the bottom shelf so that the kiddies could get them."

The fact that these messages have been translated into many languages for radio broadcasting and have been received with enthusiasm reveals the need for a simple teaching of the whole Bible for the masses of the world.

I am indebted to many people and to many sources for bringing this volume into existence. I should express my especial thanks to my secretary, Gertrude Cutler, who supervised the editorial work; to Dr. Elliott R. Cole, my associate, who handled all the detailed work with the publishers; and finally, to my wife Ruth for tenaciously encouraging me from the beginning to put my notes and messages into printed form.

Solomon wrote, ". . . of making many books there is no end; and much study is a weariness of the flesh" (Eccl. 12:12). On a sea of books that flood the marketplace, we launch this series of THRU THE BIBLE with the hope that it might draw many to the one Book, The Bible.

J. VERNON McGEE

1 THESSALONIANS

The First Epistle to the

THESSALONIANS

INTRODUCTION

This wonderful epistle is almost at the end of Paul's epistles as far as their arrangement in the New Testament is concerned. However, it was actually the first epistle that Paul wrote. It was written by Paul in A.D. 52 or 53.

Thessalonica was a Roman colony. Rome had a somewhat different policy with their captured people from what many other nations have had. For example, it seems that we try to Americanize all the people throughout the world, as if that would be the ideal. Rome was much wiser than that. She did not attempt to directly change the culture, the habits, the customs, or the language of the people whom she conquered. Instead, she would set up colonies which were arranged geographically in strategic spots throughout the empire. A city which was a Roman colony would gradually adopt Roman laws and customs and ways. In the local department stores you would see the latest things they were wearing in Rome itself. Thus these colonies were very much like a little Rome. Thessalonica was such a Roman colony, and it was an important city in the life of the Roman Empire.

Thessalonica was located fifty miles west of Philippi and about one hundred miles north of Athens. It was Cicero who said, "Thessalonica is in the bosom of the empire." It was right in the center or the heart of the empire and was the chief city of Macedonia.

The city was first named Therma because of the hot springs in that area. In 316 B.C. Cassander, one of the four generals who divided up the empire of Alexander the Great, took Macedonia and made Thessalonica his home base. He renamed the city in memory of his wife,

Thessalonike, who was a half sister of Alexander. The city is still in existence and is now known as Salonika.

The church in Thessalonica, established on Paul's second missionary journey, was a model church. Paul mentions this in the first chapter; "So that ye were ensamples to all that believe in Macedonia and Achaia" (1 Thess. 1:7). This church was a testimony to the whole area that we would call Greece today. Paul also speaks of this church as being an example to the Corinthians in 2 Corinthians 8:1-5.

You will recall that Paul and Barnabas separated prior to the second missionary journey. Paul took Silas with him, and along the route he picked up Timothy and Dr. Luke. He revisited the churches in Galatia and then attempted to make a wider circle in the densely populated area of Asia Minor, known as Turkey today. I think he intended to carry on his missionary work there, because in his third missionary journey he did make Ephesus his headquarters and did what was probably his greatest missionary work. But on his second missionary journey, the Spirit of God put up a roadblock and would not let him go south. He attempted to go up into Bithynia, but again the Spirit of God prevented him. He couldn't go north, and he couldn't go south. So he moved to the west and came to Troas to await orders. He had the vision of the man of Macedonia, so he crossed over to Philippi. He found that the man of Macedonia was instead a woman by the name of Lydia, a seller of purple—she probably ran a department store there. Paul led her to the Lord along with others of the city. Thus, a church was established at Philippi.

Then Paul went to Thessalonica, and we are told in chapter 17 of Acts that he was there for three Sabbaths. So Paul was there a little less than a month, but in that period of time he did a herculean task of mission work. Paul was an effective missionary—he led multitudes to Christ there. And in that brief time he not only organized a local church, but he also taught them the great doctrines of the Christian faith.

Now Paul had to leave Thessalonica posthaste due to great opposition to the gospel. He was run out of town and went down to Berea. The enemy pursued him to Berea, and again Paul was forced to leave. Paul left Silas and Timothy at Berea, but he went on to Athens. After some time at Athens, he went on to Corinth. Apparently it was at Corinth that Timothy and Silas came to him and brought him word concerning the Thessalonians (see 1 Thess. 3:6). Timothy also brought some questions to Paul, problems troubling the believers in Thessalonica. Paul wrote this first epistle in response to their questions, to instruct them further and give them needed comfort.

Although Paul had been in Thessalonica less than a month, he had touched on many of the great doctrines of the church, including the second coming of Christ. It is interesting that Paul did not consider this subject to be above the heads of the new converts. Yet there are churches today that have been in existence for more than one hundred years whose members have but a vague understanding of the rapture of the church and the coming of Christ to establish His Kingdom here on earth. The Thessalonian church was not even a month old, and Paul was teaching them these great doctrines!

The apostle obviously had emphasized the second coming of Christ for believers and had taught that the return of Christ was imminent; for during the period of time since Paul had left, some of the saints who had come to know and believe in Christ Jesus had died, and this had naturally raised the question in the minds of the Thessalonians as to whether these saints would be in the Rapture or not. Paul presents the second coming of Christ in relationship to believers as a *comfort*, and this forms the theme of the epistle. This emphasis is in sharp contrast to Christ's catastrophic and cataclysmic coming in glory to establish His Kingdom by putting down all unrighteousness, as seen in Revelation 19:11–16.

The epistle has a threefold purpose: (1) To *confirm* young converts in the elementary truth of the gospel; (2) to *condition* them to go on unto holy living; and (3) to *comfort* them regarding the return of Christ. Paul's message offered a marked contrast to the paganism and heathenism which were present in Thessalonica. A heathen inscription in Thessalonica read: "After death no reviving, after the grave no meeting again."

In 1 Thessalonians the emphasis is upon the rapture of believers, the coming of Christ to take His church out of the world. The fact that the coming of Christ is a purifying hope should lead to sanctification in our lives. There are a lot of people today who want to argue prophecy, and there is a great deal of curiosity about it. But John tells us, "And every man that hath this hope in him purifieth himself, even as he is pure" (1 John 3:3). This hope should have a purifying effect in our lives. I am not interested in how enthusiastic and excited you get over the truth of the rapture of the church; I want to know how you are living. Does this hope get right down to where you are living, and does it change your life?

In 2 Thessalonians the emphasis shifts to the coming of Christ to the earth to establish His Kingdom. There is a great deal of difference in our being caught up to meet the Lord in the air and His coming *down* to the earth to establish His Kingdom. I think there is a lot of upside down theology today. We need to make a distinction between our being caught up and His coming *down*.

OUTLINE

I. **The Christian's Attitude toward the Return of Christ, Chapter 1**
   to serve . . . to wait . . . vv. 9–10

II. **The Christian's Reward at the Return of Christ, Chapter 2**

III. **The Christian's Life and the Return of Christ, Chapters 3:1—4:12**

IV. **The Christian's Death and the Return of Christ, Chapter 4:13–18**

V. **The Christian's Actions in View of the Return of Christ, Chapter 5**
   Note twenty-two specific commands to Christians, beginning at v. 11

For this book we are suggesting two outlines. Each one gives a needed emphasis that is not in the other.

I. **Coming of Christ Is an Inspiring Hope, Chapter 1**
   A. Introduction, Chapter 1:1–4
   B. Gospel Received in Much Assurance and Much Affliction, Chapter 1:5–7
   C. Gospel Results: Turned from Idols to God; Wait for Coming of Christ, Chapter 1:8–10

II. **Coming of Christ Is a Working Hope, Chapter 2**
   A. Motive and Method of a True Witness for Christ, Chapter 2:1–6
   B. Mother Side of the Apostle's Ministry (Comfort), Chapter 2:7–9

CHAPTER 1

THEME: The coming of Christ is an inspiring hope

INTRODUCTION

Paul, and Silvanus, and Timotheus, unto the church of the Thessalonians which is in God the Father and in the Lord Jesus Christ: Grace be unto you, and peace, from God our Father, and the Lord Jesus Christ [1 Thess. 1:1].

This introduction is typical of Paul's other epistles, but there are some differences to which we need to call attention. Paul joins Silas and Timothy with himself in his greeting. Remember that Silas and Timothy had just returned to Paul with their report from Thessalonica. By joining their names with his, the Thessalonians would know they are all in agreement concerning this letter.

Also, Paul reveals his humility when he joins these men with himself. Silas and Timothy would have been unknown had not Paul associated himself with them. This is a very noble gesture on the part of Paul. He is always identifying himself with the brethren. He was not aloof, separated, and segregated above all the others who were working for the Lord Jesus.

This is something we need to remember today in regard to the ministry. Don't put your preacher on a pedestal; let him be right down among you. Those of us who are ministers are largely responsible for trying to make a difference between the clergy and laity. When I entered the ministry, I bought a Prince Albert coat with a long coattail. I wore a wing collar and a very white shirtfront and either a white or a black necktie. When I stood up in the pulpit, I looked like one of those little mules looking over a whitewashed fence, and I felt like one when I wore that garb! One day it came to me how ridiculous it was for me to dress differently from the officers and members of my church. None of them wore a robe or a Prince Albert coat, and I was no different from any of them. I don't think that God is asking me to live any differently either. However, when I am teaching the Word of God, I am to be very conscious of the fact that I'm giving out His Word and actually acting in His behalf, and He expects that of everyone who gives out His Word. But as far as living is concerned, God expects all of us to live on a very high plane; the life of the teacher or minister is to be no different from the life of every believer in Christ Jesus.

I wish we could eliminate this distinction between the clergy and the laity. According to the Word of God, it is a false distinction. God has a very high standard of living for all of us. I am frank to say that a paid ministry has been the curse of the church, although I don't think it could have been done otherwise in this day of specialization. However, we need to recognize that the heresies of the church have come in through a paid ministry.

There are two situations in the church which are dangerous. One is a minister who tries to exalt himself. The other is a layman who tries to be an authority on the Bible and has not really studied the Bible but has gone off on a tangent. The greatest discipline for me has been to teach the total Word of God. If a person will teach the *total* Word of God, he will deal with every subject in the Bible—he will be forced to play every key on the organ and to pull out every stop. It isn't possible to ride one hobbyhorse and emphasize one theme to the exclusion of all others if one teaches the entire Bible. I wish we had that kind of discipline in our churches today. I wish every church would go through the entire Bible.

"Unto the church of the Thessalonians which is in God the Father and in the Lord Jesus Christ." They may have a little different life-style and have different problems from the church in Philippi, but, just like the church in Philippi, it is *in* God the Father and *in* the Lord Jesus Christ. We don't read that in his other epistles because this is the first epistle Paul has written. He says it only once, and this will be enough. He won't go over this again. When the Lord Jesus prayed to the Father, He asked, "That they all may be one; as thou, Father, art in me, and I in thee, that they also may be one in us: that the world may believe that thou hast sent me. And the glory which thou gavest me I have given them; that they may be one, even as we are one: I in them, and thou in me, that they may be made perfect in one . . ." (John 17:21–23). Any believer who is in Christ Jesus is also in God the Father. That is a very safe place to be, safer than any safety deposit box!

"Grace be unto you, and peace, from God our Father, and the Lord Jesus Christ" is a formal introduction which Paul uses in all of his epistles. Grace comes first, followed by the peace of God. Both the grace and the peace come from God the Father and from the Lord Jesus Christ.

> **We give thanks to God always for you all, making mention of you in our prayers [1 Thess. 1:2].**

Paul prayed for all of the churches that he had founded. Paul had a tremendous prayer list, and it would make an interesting study for you to find all the people who were on that list. You would be surprised how many different churches, individuals, and groups of people Paul prayed for.

"We give thanks to God always for you all." Paul gives thanks for this church because of many things, and one of the most important was because they were an example; it was a model church.

The next verse is one of the most remarkable in the Bible, and it follows a pattern of the apostle Paul which we find in his writing. He emphasized the number three.

> **Remembering without ceasing your work of faith, and labour of love, and patience of hope in our Lord Jesus Christ, in the sight of God and our Father [1 Thess. 1:3].**

"Remembering without ceasing [1] your work of faith, [2] and labour of love, [3] and patience of hope in our Lord Jesus Christ."

This is a very important verse of Scripture and contains a wealth of meaning. Paul associates the three Christian graces: faith and love and hope. In 1 Corinthians he also brought these three graces together. "And now abideth faith, hope, love, these three; but the greatest of these is love" (1 Cor. 13:13).

In New Jersey several years ago I had lunch with the scientist who had designed the heat shield that was on the space capsules to protect them when they go out into space and then reenter our atmosphere. He remarked to me, "Have you ever noticed that the universe is divided into a trinity?"

"No, what do you mean by that?"

"You and I live in a physical universe that is divided into time, space, and matter. Can you think of a fourth?"

I couldn't think of any, so he continued, "Time is divided into three parts: past, present, and future. Can you think of a fourth?"

Again I couldn't, so he went on. "Space is divided into length and breadth and height. They speak of a 'fourth dimension,' but it doesn't happen to be in this material universe."

You can see that this universe in which you and I live bears the mark of the Trinity. The interesting thing is that the Word of God does the same thing. Paul speaks of man as a trinity. We will discuss this specifically when we get into the fifth chapter, verse 23: ". . . and I pray God your whole spirit and soul and body be preserved blameless unto the coming of our Lord Jesus Christ." This tells us that man is a trinity.

There are some other interesting examples of the significance of the number three. For example, have you noticed that in Genesis only three sons of Adam are named? I am sure that Adam and Eve had more than three sons; they probably had one hundred or more—they started the human race—but only three of the sons are named: Cain, Abel, and Seth.

In this verse Paul actually gives three graces of the Christian life. The past is the work of faith. The present is a labor of love. The future is the patience of hope. That is the biography of the Christian and the abiding, permanent, and eternal features of the Christian life.

Faith, hope, and love are abstract nouns. They seem to be way up yonder, but we are way down here. How can we get them out of space and theory into the reality of life down here? How can we make them concrete instead of abstract qualities?

This is like the story of the contractor who loved children. He put down a sidewalk one day—finished it in the afternoon. He came back the next morning to find that some children had walked on the concrete and had left their footmarks in it. He was very angry and was talking very loudly. A man who was standing by said, "I thought you loved children." The contractor said, "I love them in the abstract but not in the concrete!"

So the question here is how we are going to get these words down into something concrete. Paul takes these three words from the "beautiful isle of somewhere" and puts them into shoe leather. He gets them down to where the shoe leather meets the sidewalks of our hometown. He fleshes up these abstract qualities by taking them out of the morgue of never-never land.

Notice how he does it. From the "work of faith," the "labour of love," and the "patience of hope," he cites the three steps in the lives of the Thessalonian believers: "How ye turned to God from idols"— that's the work of faith; "to serve the living and true God," a labor of love; "to wait for his Son from heaven" is the patience of hope.

Now the "work of faith" is a strange expression because we are told that ". . . by grace are ye saved through faith; and that not of yourselves: it is the gift of God: Not of works, lest any man should boast" (Eph. 2:8–9). Yet here it is called the work of faith. I think that Paul is making it very clear that he and James do not contradict each other. James writes, "Yea, a man may say, Thou hast faith, and I have works: shew me thy faith without thy works, and I will shew thee my faith by my works" (James 2:18). That is the work of faith. It is the way faith is demonstrated to others. (The writings of James and the writings of Paul certainly do not contradict each other—as some have suggested—because they are both writing about the same thing.)

Faith is the response of the soul of man to the Word of God. When a man responds to the Word of God, then he walks by faith. Paul says this in 2 Corinthians 5:7: "For we walk by faith, not by sight." The Lord Jesus said the same thing: "Then said they unto him, What shall we do, that we might work the works of God? Jesus answered and said unto them, This is the work of God, that ye believe on him whom he hath sent" (John 6:28–29). He didn't say that you can come to God with your works, but that you must come to God by *faith*. Then a faith that is living will make itself manifest; it will reveal itself in the life that is lived.

There is a good illustration of this in the life of the disciples, as recorded in Luke 5:4–5. The Lord Jesus said to Simon Peter, ". . . Launch out into the deep, and let down your nets for a draught. And Simon answering said unto him, Master, we have toiled all the night, and have taken nothing." That is a statement of fact, a declaration of naked truth: "We fished all night, and we caught nothing. We know this sea, and there is no use going back out there." But notice what Simon Peter adds, "Nevertheless at thy word I will let down the net." He says he will go back and fish again. My friend, that is the work of faith. As believers we need to realize that the work of faith is acting upon the Word of God. What is the work of God? It is to believe on Jesus Christ—that is how the Lord Jesus defined it: ". . . This is the work of God, that ye believe on him whom he hath sent" (John 6:29). When you act on what the Word of God says, your faith will be evident to the world. That is the work of faith.

We have the same thing illustrated in the life of Cain and Abel. What was the problem with Cain? He was a sinner by nature, but he was also a sinner by choice and act. We are told, "By faith Abel offered unto God a more excellent sacrifice than Cain, by which he obtained witness that he was righteous . . ." (Heb. 11:4). How? By being a nice little Sunday school boy? No. Although he was a sinner as Cain was a sinner, Abel responded to the Word of God, and he believed God. When he believed God, he was saved. He manifested that faith by bringing the proper sacrifice. Faith is the connection between the believer and God. It communicates His Word to your heart and you respond. And that is what conversion is. Conversion is to believe God.

These Thessalonians turned to God from idols. Paul didn't go into Thessalonica and say, "I don't think it is proper for you people to worship idols. That's a terrible thing to do." He never said anything like that. When he went there he preached Christ! Idolatry wasn't repulsive to these people, but when they heard Paul present Christ, they believed God and they turned to God. When they turned to God, they automatically turned from idols.

People often say to me, "You converted me." I haven't converted anyone—I can't do that! One man said to me, "You saved me many years ago, and I'll never forget you." I answered him, "I appreciate your not forgetting me, but I didn't save you. All I did was to present the Word of God. You believed the Word of God, and the Spirit of God did a work in your heart." That is really quite wonderful, my friend.

Paul remembered without ceasing not only the work of faith of the Thessalonian believers but also their "labour of love." Now, what is the labor of love? God does not save by love; He saves by grace, which is love in action. Labor and love don't seem to fit together. But, you see, love will labor. And when it does, it just doesn't seem to be labor. Let me repeat the illustration of a little girl carrying a heavy baby. A man passing by said to her, "Isn't that baby too heavy for you?" She answered, "Oh no, he's my brother." Love makes all the difference in the world. Labor isn't labor when it is a labor of love.

The Lord Jesus really put it right on the line when He said, "If ye love me, keep my commandments" (John 14:15). If you don't love Him, you will find it nothing but tedium and labor to try to keep His commandments. I don't think it is worthwhile trying.

Several years ago my daughter and I were riding into Los Angeles to the church which I was pastoring. She was helping us with some work at the church. We were stuck in the traffic on the freeway, and I remarked to her, "Look at all these people going to work this morning. Notice that nobody looks happy. Everyone has a tense look on his face. They are anxious and uptight. Ninety-nine out of a hundred are going to a job they hate doing." I say it is wonderful to do what you love to do. Then it is a labor of love.

If working for the Lord is a great burden to you today, I believe the Lord Jesus would say to you, "Give it up, brother. Don't bother with it." He doesn't want it to be like that. We are to love Him. Then whatever we do for Him will be a labor of love. That should characterize the life of the believer.

One time when Dwight L. Moody came home, his family said to him, "Cancel your next meeting. You look so weary and we know you are tired." He gave this tremendous response, "I am weary in the work, but I am not weary of the work." I tell you, it is wonderful to get weary in the work of God but not to get weary of the work of God.

Love to God is expressed in obedience. I get tired of all this talk about being a dedicated Christian. If you want to make that claim, then prove it, brother. Prove it by your love, and love manifests itself in obedience.

Now the third thing for which Paul commends the Thessalonian believers is their "patience of hope." After they had turned to God from idols to serve the living and true God, they also waited for His Son from heaven. That is the patience of hope.

Every man lives with some hope for the future. And that hope, whatever it is, will sustain him. Down through the centuries man has expressed this. Martin Luther said, "Everything that is done in the world is done by hope." Long before him Sophocles, the pagan, had written: "It is hope which maintains most of mankind." A modern man, O. S. Marden, says, "There is no medicine like hope, no incentive so great, and no tonic so powerful as expectation of something better tomorrow." The poet, Alexander Pope, wrote: "Hope springs eternal in the human breast." A statesman, Thomas Jefferson, said, "I steer my bark with hope in the head, leaving fear astern." And Carlyle, the Scottish philosopher, commented, "Man is, properly speaking, based upon hope, he has no other possession but hope, this world of his is emphatically the place of hope."

What a glorious, wonderful life it is to serve the living and true God and to wait for His Son from heaven. That is the "blessed hope." Multitudes today place their hope in man, thinking that man can resolve all his problems and bring peace and prosperity to the world. Man cannot do that. If your hope is in this world, you are chasing a will-o'-the-wisp of happiness that will shatter like a bubble when you get it in your hands. You are following a Pied Piper who is playing, "I'm forever blowing bubbles." God put man out of Paradise because man was a sinner, and man has been trying to build a paradise outside ever since. The church for years thought it was building the Kingdom of Heaven, and it was not. God wouldn't even let man live forever in sin, and we can thank Him for that. Every age comes to a time of cosmic crisis and says, "Somehow we'll work our way out." Frederick the Great, the great emperor of Germany, said, "The time I live in is a time of turmoil. My hope is in God." What is your hope today? Is your hope in some political party or in some man-made organization? God have mercy on anyone whose hope rests upon some little, frail bark that man is paddling! I don't think that any man or any party or any group down here can work out the problems of this world. The sceptre of this universe is in nail-pierced hands, and He will move at the right time. This one thing I know: all things do work together for good to them who love God, to them who are the called according to His eternal and holy purpose (see Rom. 8:28).

So here Paul has brought together faith and love and hope, the three tenses of the Christian life: the work of faith, which looks back to the Cross and produces good works in the life; the labor of love, which is the present basis and motivation on which a child of God is to serve Christ; and the patience of hope, which looks into the future.

What a wonderful trinity of Christian graces! It should be the biography of every believer. It was the biography of the church in Thessalonica, and I hope it is the biography of your church too.

Now Paul takes up another great truth—

Knowing, brethren beloved, your election of God [1 Thess. 1:4].

Here we come again to that word *election*. I dealt with this when I taught Ephesians: "According as he hath chosen us in him before the foundation of the world, that we should be holy and without blame before him in love" (Eph. 1:4). Afterward I received some letters criticizing me for being weak in emphasizing election, claiming that I had soft-pedaled it; others wrote that I was rather extreme and had gone too far in talking about it. Since I got both reactions, I came to the conclusion it must have been about right. I knew it couldn't have been both extremes; so it must have been somewhere in the middle, which must be close to accurate.

Paul doesn't mind writing about election in this epistle to the Thessalonian believers. And he presents it from God's side of the ledger. You and I do not see His side, and we have never seen it. But there are certain great axioms of truth that we must put down. When I studied plane geometry, certain axioms were stated without being proven, such as the shortest distance between two points is a straight line. I have never had an occasion to dispute it, but nobody has ever attempted to prove it to me, although there is a proposition in geometry that will prove it. Nevertheless, there are certain things that we accept as fact without proof. And one of the things is the fact that there are certain things which *cannot* be proven to be true. Likewise Paul doesn't attempt to argue election or to prove election; he simply states it as a fact. "Knowing, brethren beloved, your election of God." That is God's side of the picture.

The Creator has His sovereign right. Dr. Albert Hyma, of the University of Michigan, said that for the past fifty years America has been under the control of men who do not know the origin and the beginning of our nation. They do not realize that the Puritans had a tremendous impact upon this nation. One of the great truths that the Puritans stood for, and which was basic to their entire life-style, was the sovereignty of God. Behind election and all of life is the sovereignty of God. The Creator has His sovereign right.

We need to recognize that God created the universe. I'm not concerned with *how* He did it, nor am I concerned with the account in Genesis. I simply want to emphasize the fact that in the beginning God created the heaven and the earth.

Now there are those who are willing to say He created, but they deny Him the right to *direct* the universe. They deny Him the right to give a purpose to it. May I say to you that we live in a universe that was created by God and exists for His glory. Even in the Sermon on the Mount the Lord Jesus Christ said, "Let your light so shine before men, that they may see your good works, and glorify your Father which is in heaven" (Matt. 5:16). He didn't say your good works were to glorify *yourself*. Oh, no! They are to glorify the Father in heaven. May I say especially to you, my Christian friend, that God is the Creator, and this universe exists for His glory. He is God, and beside Him there is none other. He doesn't look to anybody for advice. He is running this universe for His own purpose. He is directing it for His own glory. You and I live in a universe which is theocentric, that is, God-centered. It is not anthropocentric, man-centered; nor is it geocentric, earth-centered; but it is uranocentric, heaven-centered. This is God's universe, and He is running it His way.

Something else needs to be said: God is no tyrant. God is righteous. God is just. God is holy. Everything that God does is right. You may not always think so, but I have news for you. If you do not think God is right in what He is doing, and if you think that God is not following the best plan, the news I have for you is that you are *wrong*. God is not wrong. You are wrong. You are the person who needs to get his thinking corrected, because if you don't, you are out of step with the universe. This universe exists for God, for His glory, and for His purpose. There is nothing going to happen that will not work out to His glory. He is in charge, and He is running this universe today.

With this in mind, let's consider something else. Have you ever stopped to consider the fact that you were *born*? You could have been nonexistent. I could have been nonexistent. God did not come to me and ask, "Vernon McGee, do you want to come into existence?" I wasn't even in existence so that He could ask me! *He* is the One who thought of it. He is the One who is responsible for my existence. And He did not ask me whether I wanted to be male or female. He didn't ask me whether I wanted to be born in this day and age. He didn't ask me to choose my parents. He didn't ask me to decide whether my parents would be godly or whether they would be wealthy—and they were neither one. God today is running this universe because it is His. You may not like it, but that just happens to be the way it is.

Now God is no tyrant—no one is chosen against his will, and no one is rejected against his will. God is right in all that He does. Paul asks, "What shall we say then? Is there unrighteousness with God?" And he answers his own question with a strong negative, "God forbid" (Rom. 9:14). God is right in all that He does.

We need to get back to that place where we recognize that we are mere creatures. Not only creatures, but we are totally depraved creatures. I know it's not popular to say this in our day. We like to scratch each other's backs and tell each other how wonderful we are. That's the reason they hand out loving cups, and these knife-and-fork clubs are always recognizing somebody as the outstanding something or other. The human race must do that in order to bolster us up and make us think that we are great down here. The fact is that we are in rebellion against God.

The fact that God even considers us as a nation is due to the early Puritans who founded this country. They are being downgraded in our day, but we have this great country because of them. Other men have labored, and we have entered into their labors. And one of the things that they emphasized was the liberty of each individual for private judgment. Even we as sinners have that right. Why? Because no other sinner has any right to make a decision for you and me. Today you and I enjoy the freedom that we have because of our Puritan forefathers. The present generation of politicians doesn't even know what it's all about, which is the reason democracy isn't working. There is no way democracy can work unless the people understand the sovereignty of God, recognize they are His creatures, and fall down before Him.

Now let me repeat what Paul has said to the Thessalonian believers (v. 4): "Knowing, brethren beloved, your election of God." Maybe you don't like this verse, but this is the way it happened. And God is running this universe. Instead of joining a protest march against Him, I suggest that you fall down on your face before Him and thank Him that He has brought you into existence, and that He has given you the opportunity as a free moral agent to make a decision for Him. His invitation still stands, ". . . If any man thirst, let him come unto me, and drink" (John 7:37). Are you thirsty? Then come to Christ. He stands ready to receive you. You say you are not thirsty? Then forget it. God offers a full and free salvation to this lost world today. He says to men and women, "Take it or leave it." That is where our freedom comes in. We can either choose Him or reject Him. There is no middle ground. Each person has the freedom to do one or the other.

GOSPEL RECEIVED IN MUCH ASSURANCE AND MUCH AFFLICTION

Now here is another tremendous verse for us to study—

For our gospel came not unto you in word only, but also in power, and in the Holy Ghost, and in much assur-

**ance; as ye know what manner of men we were among
you for your sake [1 Thess. 1:5].**

Paul is saying, "You knew that when we came among you, we were
just human beings—just weak human beings with lips and tongues of
clay. All we could do was say words, but we gave out the Word of God.
And the Word of God came to you, not in word only, but in power and
in the Holy Spirit." My friend, this fact makes my job the most wonderful job in the world. I love it. I love to teach the Word of God. Do
you know why? Because when I give out the Word of God—although
they are just words as far as Vernon McGee is concerned—when the
Spirit of God takes those words and uses them, they are *powerful!* I
suppose I have about five hundred letters on my desk right now that
bear this out. For example, a wife has written that the first time she
turned on my radio program, her husband spent thirty minutes cuss-
ing this preacher. But she continued to tune in the program, and one
day he argued back at me. Then one day she forgot to dial in the program and he reminded her of it, and he listened. Finally the day came
when he knelt by the radio and received Christ as his Savior! My
friend, if you think that happened because I am a super-duper salesman, you are wrong. I'm not even a salesman—I couldn't even give
away five-dollar bills, because folk would think they were phony! But
the thing that is so tremendous is that the Spirit of God will use the
Word of God. That is our confidence.

Now hear me carefully: I believe that the Bible is the inerrant Word
of God. And please don't write to me and explain to me all the intro-
ductions and all the problems about text. I've been through seminary,
and I have even taught introductory courses so that I do know a little
about them. But I accept the Word of God as the inerrant Word of God,
that it is God speaking to us. And I go further than that. I believe that
the Spirit of God can cause the Word of God to penetrate into your
heart and life and my heart and life so that we are transformed people.
People are not born again by the weakness of the human flesh, not by
saying a few words by radio or by the printed page. But they are
". . . born again, not of corruptible seed, but of incorruptible, by the

word of God, which liveth and abideth for ever" (1 Pet. 1:23). I believe the Spirit of God can take the Word of God and make it *real* to you. I believe the Word of God is that kind of thing. I don't think the Spirit of God could do much with the telephone directory or the Sears and Roebuck catalog or with popular magazines that are published today. But I do believe that the Spirit of God can and will take the Word of God and perform the greatest miracle possible—changing an unbelieving, lost sinner into a child of God!

The Word of God went into Thessalonica, that Roman colony which was pagan and heathen and was controlled by one of the greatest political and military powers this world has known, and there it reached the hearts and lives of people and transformed them. That is what happened in Thessalonica, and it can still do the same today.

Let me repeat verse 5 because it is such an important verse: "For our gospel came not unto you in word only, but also in power, and in the Holy Ghost, and in much assurance; as ye know what manner of men we were among you for your sake."

The first thing necessary is for a person to *hear* the Word of God. That is the factual basis. People must hear the gospel. "So then faith cometh by hearing, and hearing by the word of God" (Rom. 10:17). That is the natural part of the process. But that doesn't end it, because the Word of God is a supernatural book. Without the Holy Spirit the gospel is merely words. With the Holy Spirit it is the power of God unto salvation to everyone that believes. This is exactly what the Lord Jesus said the Holy Spirit would do: "Nevertheless I tell you the truth; It is expedient for you that I go away: for if I go not away, the Comforter will not come unto you; but if I depart, I will send him to you. And when he is come, he will reprove the world of sin, and of righteousness, and of judgment: Of sin, because they believe not on me; Of righteousness, because I go to my Father, and ye see me no more; Of judgment, because the prince of this world is judged" (John 16:7–11).

And ye became followers of us, and of the Lord, having received the word in much affliction, with joy of the Holy Ghost [1 Thess. 1:6].

Paul could cite Silas and Timothy and himself as examples. Personally, I would hesitate to give myself as an example; I don't think I am a very good one. But Paul the apostle, going from place to place throughout the Roman Empire, offered himself as an example to these believers.

"Having received the word in much affliction, with joy of the Holy Ghost." *Affliction* (or suffering) and *joy* are two words that are actually antipodes apart—they are as far apart as the east is from the west. They don't belong together. They are as extreme as night is from daylight, as cold is from heat. They are not things that we would associate together. If a person is suffering and in affliction, he cannot have any joy, according to our natural way of looking at it. And if he's having joy in his life, then surely he isn't suffering!

Yet there have been wonderful saints of God who have endured affliction and at the same time have had the joy of the Lord in their hearts. That is real triumph. We hear a lot about healing today, and I thank God that He has healed me. How wonderful it is! But I know some saints of God who are a lot more wonderful than I ever hope to be. These people are lying right now on beds of pain, beds of affliction, and they have the joy of the Lord in their hearts.

There is not a person today who is enjoying the world's entertainment and is suffering at the same time. The world cannot put these two together. Paul says that the Word was received "in much affliction"—there was suffering, persecution, and heartache. But there was the joy of the Holy Spirit also. That is the bittersweet of life; that is like the Chinese dish they call "sweet-and-sour." For the Christian there can be that which is sour and bitter in life, while at the same time there is sweetness in the heart and life.

A woman who was a rather famous poetess here in Southern California was a member of my church. I had the privilege of baptizing her. We baptized her in a bathtub because we couldn't take her anywhere else. The minute I touched her she screamed, because she was in pain all the time. She gave me a copy of one of her last books of poetry. It was titled, *Heart Held High*. In the midst of extreme human suffering she had the joy of the Lord in her life. I always left her with the distinct feeling that I was the one who had been ministered to. I never felt that I did much ministering to her. It is wonderful to see a Christian who is suffering like that and can still rejoice in the Lord.

So that ye were ensamples to all that believe in Macedonia and Achaia [1 Thess. 1:7].

"In Macedonia and Achaia"—this refers to the European section of the Greco-Macedonian empire of Alexander the Great. The church at Thessalonica, a Roman colony, was an example—after just a few months—to all the other churches. What a glorious, wonderful testimony they had.

Today we often hear of individual Christians who are examples to others. However, there are actually very few churches which are known far and near as being examples of the Christian faith. I think it is strange that we do not have more local churches which are examples to all believers. It has been my privilege to travel around the country and speak in many churches across America. There are a few, but only a few, that I would name as examples.

GOSPEL RESULTS

For from you sounded out the word of the Lord not only in Macedonia and Achaia, but also in every place your faith to God-ward is spread abroad; so that we need not to speak any thing [1 Thess. 1:8].

Paul found that wherever he traveled the reputation of this church had already gone ahead of him. The believers were already talking about the church in Thessalonica; so it wasn't necessary for Paul to tell them anything about it. This reveals something of the great reputation this church had in that day.

For they themselves shew of us what manner of entering in we had unto you, and how ye turned to God from idols to serve the living and true God;

And to wait for his Son from heaven, whom he raised from the dead, even Jesus, which delivered us from the wrath to come [1 Thess. 1:9-10].

We have already looked at these two verses in connection with verse 3. Their response gave witness to the kind of "entering in" Paul and Silas and Timothy had had with them. Paul tells what that response was: (1) Your work of faith—how ye turned to God from idols; (2) your labor of love—to serve the living and true God; and (3) your patience of hope—to wait for His Son from heaven.

Now I would like to look at these verses from a little different point of view. When Paul arrived in Thessalonica, he did not announce that he would give a series of messages denouncing idolatry or telling about the errors that were involved in the worship of Apollo, Venus, or any of the other gods and goddesses of the Roman Empire. But when Paul arrived in Thessalonica, he preached Christ. When he preached Christ, they turned to God from idols. Notice that he doesn't say they turned from idols to God. Someone will say, "You're splitting hairs." I surely am. These are hairs that need to be split. We need to do some straight thinking about this.

"How ye turned to God from idols." We hear today that repentance is essential to salvation. Repentance and believing are presented as two steps in a process. Actually, they are both wrapped up in the same package, and you have them both right here. When Paul preached Christ, they turned *to* God *from* idols. I want you to see something that is very important. When they turned *to* God, that is the work of faith; that is what faith did. The Lord Jesus said, ". . . This is the work of God, that ye *believe* on him whom he hath sent" (John 6:29, italics mine). These people turned to God from idols; they turned *from* idols, too. That's right—and that is repentance. The repentance followed the turning to God. It didn't precede it. When they turned to God, they automatically turned from idols.

Take your hand and hold it so the palm of your hand is facing toward you. Now turn your hand around. When you turned your hand around, the back side of your hand now faces you, and the palm of your hand automatically turned away from you. Just so, you cannot turn to Christ Jesus without turning from something, my friend. That turning from something is repentance.

We need to hold up Jesus Christ as the Savior from sin. A man needs to know that he is a lost sinner. He can sit and weep about his sins until Judgment Day, and it won't do him one bit of good. I know an alcoholic man who died an alcoholic. He could sit in my study and cry about the fact that he was an alcoholic and how terrible he was to be a drunkard. He could shed great tears and repent, but nothing changed because he never did turn to Christ!

My dad used to tell about a little boat that went up and down the Mississippi River. It had a little bitty boiler and a great big whistle. When that boat was carrying a load and was going upstream, it was in trouble when the whistle would blow, because the boat would begin to drift downstream. There are a lot of people who have a little boiler and a great big whistle. They can repent and shed tears all over the place, but that doesn't do any good. It is only when a person turns to Christ that he will turn from something. He will turn from his sin. If a man doesn't turn from his sin, it is because he hasn't turned to Christ.

I am sure that when the Thessalonian believers turned from their idols, they wept over the time they had wasted in idol worship. After they had turned to God, there was a real repentance over the misspent years. The turning to God came first, then they realized that turning to God meant turning from idols.

Now I want to point out that Jesus Christ the Savior of the world is to be preached to a world of lost sinners, but the message of repentance is preached to the church. Read the messages to the seven churches of Asia as recorded in Revelation, chapters 2 and 3. The message of the Lord Jesus to the churches is to repent. Today it seems that the church is telling everyone outside the church to repent. The Bible teaches that it is the people in the church who need to repent. We need to get down on our faces before God and repent. That is not the message for us to give to the unsaved man down the street. He needs to know that he has a Savior.

"To serve the living and true God." The Thessalonians were now serving God; it was the labor of love. You cannot serve Christ unless you love Him. The Lord Jesus said, "If ye love me, keep my commandments" (John 14:15). Suppose you don't love Him? Then there are none of His commandments for you. You think you want to go out to preach the gospel, but you don't love Him? Then stay home. To go into all the world and preach the gospel to every creature is a command, and it is for those who love Him. If you don't love Him, don't do it.

When the Lord Jesus talked to Simon Peter (as recorded in John 21), He didn't ask, "Peter, why in the world did you deny Me?" He didn't say, "Peter, do you promise Me you will do better if I let you preach the sermon on the Day of Pentecost?" He never said anything like that. He asked, "Peter, do you love Me?" If Peter had said, "No," I think the Lord would have told him to forget about service. Does that sound harsh to you? I didn't say it; Jesus did: "If ye love me, keep my commandments."

"And to wait for his Son from heaven." That doesn't mean to wait sitting down. It means you are busy. If you love Him, you will serve Him. You are busy for Him while you wait for Him.

When I first went to Cleburne, Texas, all the downtown churches had outdoor evening services on the lawn of the First Baptist Church. Since I was the new preacher in town, I was asked to preach the first night I was there. An officer of one of the churches had heard that I was a fundamentalist and a premillennialist. The next day he said to me, "I heard your sermon last night. You didn't sound to me like one of those fellows who has his nose pressed against the window waiting for the Lord to come." I told him that people who are waiting for the Lord to come don't have their noses against the window. They are out, busy, working for the Lord. This was during the depression, but I told him that while his and other denominations were calling their missionaries back from the field, the China Inland Mission, which was fundamental and premillennial, was asking for one hundred more missionaries to go to China. Who was really waiting for the Lord to come?

"To wait for his Son from heaven" does not mean to sit down. It means to be busy for the Lord. That is the patience of hope. It means to keep on serving the Lord, giving out the Word of God while you wait. The coming of Christ to take His church out of the world is not an escape mechanism. Rather, it is an incentive to serve Him and to give out the Word of God. ". . . Even so, come, Lord Jesus" (Rev. 22:20).

CHAPTER 2

THEME: The coming of Christ is a working hope

The coming of Christ for His church is called the rapture of the church. It is not a doctrine to argue about; it is a doctrine to *live*. Unfortunately, there are many who believe Christ is coming after the Great Tribulation. There are those who believe He is coming before, and some believe He is coming during that period of time. Then there are others who don't believe that He is coming at all, and yet they say that they trust Him as their Savior. For all the groups there is one important question: How does your interpretation affect your life? Does it do anything for you? If your view has no effect on your life, then you should reconsider what you believe. The expectation of the return of the Lord should be a motivating factor in the life of the believer.

MOTIVE AND METHOD OF A TRUE WITNESS FOR CHRIST

For yourselves, brethren, know our entrance in unto you, that it was not in vain [1 Thess. 2:1].

"In vain" means empty, without results. Paul says, "When we came to you, it was not just some theoretical proposition that we presented to you. We didn't come to declare to you something that was new and novel and which had no effect on you at all. We didn't just entertain you for a few days and then leave you." Paul's work was not in vain; it was not empty. When he came to Thessalonica, it rocked a great many folk, bringing many to a saving knowledge of Christ. And it brought a church into existence. Paul was not simply talking about a theory or a philosophy, but about something that *worked* in Thessalonica. The gospel walked down the streets of that city, and it got into the hearts and homes and lives of men and women.

> But even after that we had suffered before, and were
> shamefully entreated, as ye know, at Philippi, we were
> bold in our God to speak unto you the gospel of God
> with much contention [1 Thess. 2:2].

The Greek word for "contention" is agoni, which means "conflict" or
"agony." There was a great deal of conflict and much inward agony
when Paul came to them.

Paul says that he had been shamefully treated in Philippi. We
know about that from the account in Acts 16. But when he came to
Thessalonica, he came in boldness. In other words, he didn't slow
down because of his previous experience. He didn't play down the
gospel. After his terrifying experience, Paul didn't say, "Now I'm going to change my approach. I'm going to be more tactful and less out-
spoken about the gospel." No, Paul was not a secret believer. He spoke
right out, just as he had done at Philippi.

You see, it would have been so easy for Paul to rationalize. He
could have decided that he had better be more careful to win friends
and influence people. Excessive tact and the soft sell were not Paul's
method. He boldly declared the gospel, and his experiences did not
affect his approach.

Now when he entered in among them, he presented the Word of
God. If you were asked to choose, what would you select as the greatest sermon of the apostle Paul? If we took a poll, I'm sure we would
get many different answers. Rightly so. There was the great sermon at
Damascus after his conversion. There was the sermon before Sergius
Paulus on the island of Cyprus when he began his missionary work.
Then there was a sermon in the synagogue at Antioch of Pisidia on his
first missionary journey—I consider that one of the greatest of his sermons. Then there were sermons in Athens on Mars Hill, in Ephesus at
the school of Tyrannus, and his defense in Corinth. I think all of these
are great. Someone might choose the message he gave in Jerusalem
when he was arrested, or when he was brought before Felix and Festus
and Agrippa. The one given before Agrippa is a masterpiece. Then
there is his farewell speech on the beach to the elders of Ephesus. In

every message he always presented Christ, His death and His resurrection.

If I were to pick the greatest sermon of Paul, I would actually pick none of these. I would choose instead *his life* in Thessalonica. His greatest sermon was not in writing or speaking, but in walking. It was not in exposition, but in experience; not in his profession, but in his practice. He took his text from James 2:26, ". . . faith without works is dead. . . ." and he made his points on the pavement of the streets of Thessalonica.

Every believer is a preacher. Maybe you don't like me to call you a preacher, but you are one nonetheless. You can't escape it—you are saying something to somebody by the life you live. Perhaps your life is speaking to the child in your home. I think that is one of the reasons we have so many of our young people out on the highways and byways, the streets and alleys of this world. They watched mom and dad at home, and they didn't like what they saw; so they took to the highways. The greatest sermon you will ever preach is by the life that you live.

Paul is going to tell us about the sermon he preached at Thessalonica (vv. 3–6), and he then will describe the relationship he had with the Thessalonians. He was like a *mother* to them in that he comforted them (see v. 7); he was like a *father* to them in that he charged them (v. 11); and he was like a *brother* to the Thessalonians in that he challenged them (v. 14).

For our exhortation was not of deceit, nor of uncleanness, nor in guile [1 Thess. 2:3].

Deceit means "error." The content of Paul's exhortation was not adulterated. Paul did not water down the gospel. He never changed it to suit different groups.

One of the things that disturbs me about some ministers is that they give a good, clearcut gospel message in one place, but then they show up in another place where they need to be equally clear in giving out the gospel, and they are fuzzy! This was not true of the apostle Paul—his "exhortation was not of deceit."

Uncleanness means "sensuality." Paul was not motivated by greed. He didn't come to Thessalonica for the offering he would get or for the notoriety he would gain. He wasn't seeking to be ministered to personally, but he came with pure motives. There was no uncleanness in that sense.

"Nor in guile"—he did not use wrong methods with them. He did not lower his standards to accommodate the prejudices and passions of the old nature. He did not use an appeal to the sinful flesh.

Many of us can learn a lesson from the apostle Paul at this point. I once knew a minister who had been a great preacher. But I lost much respect for this man because he went back to a church which he had formerly pastored, knowing that there was criticism of the present pastor. He played upon that criticism and encouraged it. Paul would never have done a thing like that. He didn't bring the gospel to people in any form of guile at all.

Everyone who teaches the Word of God needs to ask himself whether he is doing it with any deceit or uncleanness or guile. We need to be honest with ourselves; we need to check our own motives. Do we teach in order to win friends and influence people? Or are we honestly trying to give out the Word of God? My friend, I must confess that I have made many mistakes. I have failed the Lord so many times that it is amazing that He doesn't throw me overboard. If I were God, I would have been disgusted with Vernon McGee long ago. But I promised the Lord when I entered the ministry that I wouldn't pull any punches. Honestly, I expected to get into real trouble, but the Lord has been good to me. I think He knew that I would start running if there were an occasion for it. I am grateful that I can look up to the Lord right now and say, "Lord, I've made a lot of mistakes and I have failed You, but I have given out Your Word the best I know how. If I could give it better, I would, but I'm doing the best that I possibly can by Your grace."

I love this passage. Paul could tell the Thessalonians, "When I came to you, I want you to know that I had no ulterior motives. I didn't come for your offering. I didn't come in order to shear your sheep.

I came to give you the gospel and then to build you up in the faith. That was my motive." With that kind of motive a person is really sailing on a marvelous sea. There may be storms, but the Lord will bring His servant through.

> **But as we were allowed of God to be put in trust with the gospel, even so we speak; not as pleasing men, but God, which trieth our hearts [1 Thess. 2:4].**

The word *allowed* means "to be tested or approved." Paul was saying that he was no novice. He was not a manpleaser, nor had he ever sought popularity. He wasn't trying to make a name for himself. When Paul preached, he was not preaching to find out what men would think of him, but what God would think of him. Paul used the blue litmus paper of God to put down in his life, and it stood the test. He never used any low or tricky methods.

> **For neither at any time used we flattering words, as ye know, nor a cloak of covetousness; God is witness [1 Thess. 2:5].**

Paul is speaking pretty frankly. He says that he never came into their midst to flatter anyone. He never played up to the rich people in the congregation. He didn't try to butter up anyone.

Flattery disarms us—we really never know what to say. When people criticize me, I know what to say, but I never know what to say when someone flatters me. It disarms a person. In *Twelfth Night* Shakespeare has his clown say, "Marry, sir, they praise me and make an ass of me; now my foes tell me plainly I am an ass: so that by my foes, sir, I profit in the knowledge of myself, and by my friends I am abused." Our friends are probably more dangerous at times than our enemies!

Paul never used flattery. There is a group of wealthy laymen across this country who are literally owned by the people who flatter them. If a Christian work or program doesn't butter them up, they are not the least bit interested in helping that program financially. God pity the church or the work that must depend on men who require flattery and compliments before they will give their support to the work. I think this is one of the curses in the Christian church today.

Paul did not use a "cloak of covetousness." I really don't think that money is the sin of the ministry. I have never felt that money was a great temptation for the men whom I know in the ministry. But the cloak of covetousness is a cloak of many colors. There are men who covet honor and fame and position. We need to search our hearts in order to uncover any covetousness there.

Many colleges have attempted to buy men by giving them honorary doctoral degrees. They have been given out by the score. The college then hopes for a donation or some other type of support. That is one reason it would be well if all doctoral degrees had to be earned.

> **Nor of men sought we glory, neither of you, nor yet of others, when we might have been burdensome, as the apostles of Christ [1 Thess. 2:6].**

Paul never sought position or honors. He never received any honorary degrees. He had pure motives.

THE MOTHER SIDE OF THE APOSTLE'S MINISTRY (COMFORT)

> **But we were gentle among you, even as a nurse cherisheth her children [1 Thess. 2:7].**

The word nurse here means "a nursing mother," like a mother bird. This is Paul's positive expression of his relationship to the Thessalonians: "I've been a nursing mother, a mother bird to you." Oh, the gentleness of Paul! He was as tender as a woman in his dealings with the church at Thessalonica.

The Lord Jesus said of Jerusalem: "O Jerusalem, Jerusalem, thou that killest the prophets, and stonest them which are sent unto thee, how often would I have gathered thy children together, even as a hen gathereth her chickens under her wings, and ye would not!" (Matt.

23:37). Jesus identifies Himself in many ways in Scripture. He calls Himself the Good Shepherd who gave His life for the sheep. He protects His sheep, and someday He is going to gather them all into a fold where they will be safe with Him. Then He also uses this idea of the mother hen with her little chicks.

I was raised in the country, and I remember that in the spring of the year we would put an old setting hen on some eggs. Soon she had a little flock of chicks. She would go all around the yard clucking. We didn't have a special chicken yard because we lived on a great big place by a cotton gin, and these chickens would roam over an area about a quarter mile square. When the rain would come, the mother hen would cluck, cluck, cluck, calling her chicks to the hen house. Sometimes they wouldn't quite make it; so the mother hen would get all those little chicks under her, and she would cover them with her feathers. The rain would be running down off her, but all the little ones were safe under her wings. How many times the Lord Jesus says to us, "Just come in under My wings."

Paul was that kind of minister. He loved the Thessalonians with a mother's love. They were dear to him. There are still ministers like that today. Maybe they aren't all great expositors, but they believe the Word of God and preach it. Such godly and experienced pastors are able to counsel people who are in need of help. You don't need to be afraid to sit down and open your heart to such a man and let him help you.

> **So being affectionately desirous of you, we were willing to have imparted unto you, not the gospel of God only, but also our own souls, because ye were dear unto us [1 Thess. 2:8].**

Dear is "beloved." Paul had a genuine love for the Thessalonian believers, and he was willing literally to give his life for them.

> **For ye remember, brethren, our labour and travail: for labouring night and day, because we would not be chargeable unto any of you, we preached unto you the gospel of God [1 Thess. 2:9].**

"Travail . . . labouring night and day"—that's a mother's work. We are familiar with the expression: "Man's work is from sun to sun, but a woman's work [or a mother's work] is never done." A mother is not a paid nurse. Paul is saying that he wasn't a paid nurse who worked by the hour. He wasn't a hired babysitter. He did not belong to a union.

Have you ever heard of a mothers' union which insisted a mother would work only for eight hours of the day? Have you known any mothers who punch the clock and then turn away from their crying babies because they refuse to work anymore? Maybe some mothers will work out some kind of union agreement like that, but I don't think *real* mothers would want it. Mothers work a little differently— night and day.

In New England there were two girls who worked together in the cotton mills. One of them quit working, and they didn't see each other for several years. They met on the street one day, and the girl from the mill said, "What are you doing now? Are you still working?" The other one replied, "No, I'm not working—I'm married. I not only have a husband, but I also have a little boy. I get up at three in the morning to feed the baby. Then I get up early to fix breakfast and make a lunch for my husband. I take care of the baby through the day, and then I prepare dinner for my husband." The first girl exclaimed, "I remember when you worked at the mill how you used to watch the clock. When that five o'clock whistle blew, you were out of there!" The young mother explained: "I don't watch the clock anymore. I'm working longer hours, but it isn't really work." This girl was motivated by love, and it didn't seem like work anymore.

That is what Paul is saying here. He loved these people. He labored over them night and day because he loved them.

A member of my church once asked me to go visit someone. He said, "You're *paid* to do that." Do you know what I told him? I said, "*You* go to see him—because you are not paid to do it, and you will probably do a better job than I could do. We are not to do the Lord's work on the basis of *pay!*" I'm afraid that put him in an awkward position. He had to make that call, and I can assure you, he never asked that of me again. We are to care for one another with the tender care of a mother. That was what Paul did.

THE FATHER SIDE OF THE APOSTLE'S MINISTRY
(CHARGE)

Ye are witnesses, and God also, how holily and justly and unblameably we behaved ourselves among you that believe [1 Thess. 2:10].

"Ye are witnesses"—Paul is speaking of something which they know to be true. Notice the way Paul conducted himself among them.

"Holily"—he carefully discharged his duty to God. That is what holy living is. "Justly"—he also carefully discharged his duty to man. Paul had a duty to God and a duty to man; he discharged both of them.

I hear so many people talk about being "dedicated Christians." If you hope to be a dedicated Christian, you must live a holy life before God. Watch God, and don't watch the clock. Don't work only when the boss is around. You should work all the time, because God is always around. Going down front in a church service, shedding a few tears, and having someone pray over you will not produce a dedicated life. What does your *boss* think of you? Or if you are a student, what does your teacher think of you? If you are lazy, then you are not dedicated. A dedicated life is a holy life, lived always in the presence of God.

"Unblameably." This means that no charge could be maintained against the apostle and his companions. This doesn't mean that his enemies didn't accuse him—because they did—but the charges didn't stick.

People will say ugly things about you, but the important thing is to make sure the criticisms are not true. Paul and his companions maintained a holy life. A holy life does count. It has nothing to do with obtaining your salvation, but it has everything to do with the salvation of folk around you, because they are watching you.

As ye know how we exhorted and comforted and charged every one of you, as a father doth his children [1 Thess. 2:11].

"Exhorted." The Greek word is *parakaleo*, which means that Paul came to the side of them to help, to entreat, and to convict them. It is the same word which is used for the Holy Spirit. You remember that the Lord Jesus said he would send the Holy Spirit who would convict the world of sin, of righteousness, and of judgment (see John 16:7–11).

I have always felt that the gospel is not presented in the power of the Holy Spirit unless it is presented as something that the Holy Spirit can use to convict a man. That means that He convinces a man of sin, of righteousness, and of judgment. Those three elements are always in the gospel message.

Comforted is not used here in the sense we use the word today. We saw that meaning on the mother side of the apostle's ministry. Rather, the word here means "to persuade." There was an urgency in Paul's message to the Thessalonians. He often said, "I beseech you"—I beg you. That is the way the gospel should be presented even today.

Paul "charged" them. This has a note of severity in it—it involves discipline. It is a virile word, a robust, firm, masculine word. I'm afraid that we find a lot of sissy preaching in our pulpits today. The popular thing is to have a little sermonette given by a preacherette to Christianettes. There is little urgency. Someone has defined the average church service in a liberal church as when a mild-mannered man gets up before a group of mild-mannered people and urges them to be more mild-mannered. Oh, that is sickening, my friend!

My wife says that I indulge my flesh at Eastertime because I just have to laugh when I look through the paper and see what the liberal preachers are going to preach for the Resurrection. They have a problem with that. And I enjoy their discomfort! One preacher's subject was given as "Easter Is a Time of Flowers." Oh boy, don't you imagine that was a virile, robust sermon? No wonder there are so many sick saints when they are being fed such watered down soup. A great Methodist evangelist in the South once said, "Some sermons don't have enough gospel in them to make soup for a sick grasshopper." In contrast, what a glorious thing the ministry of the apostle Paul was!

That ye would walk worthy of God, who hath called you unto his kingdom and glory [1 Thess. 2:12].

"Walk worthy." This is what Paul also wrote to the Ephesians: "I therefore, the prisoner of the Lord, beseech you that ye walk worthy of the vocation wherewith ye are called" (Eph. 4:1).

God has called the saints unto "his kingdom," which refers to the millennial kingdom, and unto "glory," which refers to the eternal kingdom. In other words, get a perspective of God's great plan and purpose. Live in the light of eternity.

> **For this cause also thank we God without ceasing, because, when ye received the word of God which ye heard of us, ye received it not as the word of men, but as it is in truth, the word of God, which effectually worketh also in you that believe [1 Thess. 2:13].**

Now here is the other side of the giving of the gospel. Paul has already said, "For our gospel came not unto you in word only, but also in power, and in the Holy Ghost . . ." (1 Thess. 1:5). That is the way the gospel should be given out. But I hear a great many people criticize preachers, and I want to say this: If a man is presenting the gospel and it is going out in power, it should also be received as the Word of God.

How do you receive the Word of God? Do you receive it as the Word of God? Or do you get angry? Does the hair stand up on the back of your neck? Twice in all my years of ministry I was approached by a man after a sermon and asked if I had him in mind when I preached the sermon that morning. My friend, I didn't even know those men were there! They were giving themselves an added sense of importance that wasn't justified. But the real issue is that they weren't receiving the Word of God as the Word of God.

The Word should go out as the Word of God and it should be received as the Word of God. And, my friend, if you will receive it that way, then it will be able to work in you, and there's blessing there for you. Otherwise, you are wasting your time in church.

We have seen how Paul has been giving out the Word of God. It irritated some people because God's Word is salt, and salt stings when it gets into a fresh wound of sin in the life of an individual. The Word of God is also a light, but there are a lot of people who love darkness because their deeds are evil.

Paul is teaching in this chapter that the church of God should mirror the family of God down here on earth. He talks about a mother relationship to believers, a father relationship, and now a brother relationship. Sometimes people say, "Our church is a family church." What they mean is that there is a nursery for the little baby, a junior church for all the little children of junior age, a teenage group, a couples' group for dad and mom, and finally a senior citizens' group for grandma and grandpa. That is what folk call a "family church." I am not sure Paul would ever have divided up the church like that, and this is not what we mean when we say the church should mirror the family of God.

The church should be a *revelation* of *God* to the community just as a family should be. The relationships of husband, wife, and child in the home should reveal the threefold aspect of the love of God and Christ for the world. Paul has already spoken of the *mother* side of the local church. He was willing to work day and night to nurture them as a little bird is nurtured by its mother. He didn't work an eight-hour day, but he was on the job for them all the time.

Then Paul says he was like a *father* to that church. A child in a home needs to experience both mother-love and father-love. It is a tragedy for children in our day when the parents are separated or divorced. The child very often fails to receive the love of the father. That father-love is expressed in discipline. Paul says he was like a father to the Thessalonian church.

There are some very fine Bible teachers who never preach anything but comfort. They are always comforting the saints. People love it, because everyone likes to be comforted. I like to have my back rubbed and my head also. That is physically comforting, and it is a joy. But we are not to have comfort alone; we also need discipline. I'm afraid that the father-side, the discipline-side, is woefully lacking, not only in our homes and in the state, but also in the church.

THE BROTHER SIDE OF THE APOSTLE'S MINISTRY (CHALLENGE)

Now the brother-side of the ministry within the church is represented by the child in the family.

> **For ye, brethren, became followers of the churches of God which in Judaea are in Christ Jesus: for ye also have suffered like things of your own countrymen, even as they have of the Jews [1 Thess. 2:14].**

"Brethren"—that is, brothers. What is it that makes men brothers? There are two things that make brothers. Regardless of race or color, it is true that we have all sinned and come short of the glory of God. No one escapes that category. This is the brotherhood of sinners. Since it is a brotherhood of sinners, it is not a loving brotherhood. You had better watch your brother; you can't always trust him.

Now what is it that Paul says drew the Thessalonians together as brothers? "For ye also have suffered like things of your own countrymen." The Thessalonian church was largely a gentile church, and they were already experiencing persecution, although this was not yet the time of the great persecutions under the emperors. They were suffering in Thessalonica. Paul could say to them, "Before you began suffering, the brethren over in Jerusalem were already suffering at the hands of their racial brothers. This suffering draws you together and holds you together." They were brothers in suffering; suffering is a cement that holds believers together.

The church is coming "unglued" in some areas of the world, and the reason for this is the same thing that was said of Israel in Deuteronomy 32:15: "Jeshurun waxed fat, and kicked." That is, they entered a period of affluence, and they became critical. The church in America lives in affluence. But, frankly, I think that persecution may be just around the corner.

There are many in the church who are praying for revival. I know of a number of prayer groups which meet regularly to pray for revival.

I have never heard of them praying that they might all suffer or be persecuted in order to bring in revival. I do not think that revival will come to this country under the present state of conditions. Right now there is a renewed interest in the Word of God, and some call it revival. However, I don't call this revival. I believe that if revival came to the church, we would all know it. No one would need to ask, "Do you think this is revival?"

But I do believe that if suffering came to the church, it would draw believers together. We would cut out all this nonsense of picking at the other fellow. We would recognize that every child of God is our brother. There may be some disagreement on various points, but every believer in the Lord Jesus Christ is my brother. We are in the family of God, and we should mirror this before the world. When the church *really* mirrors this before the world, then revival will come.

We try to make a detour and a shortcut to revival by praying for it. Why don't we pray for the *conditions* that produce revival? It was man's *extremity* that brought revival at times in the past. The great Wesleyan movement came out of the dark days in England when they were on the verge of a revolution. It seems it takes such conditions for revival to occur. Maybe we are not far from that in our country today.

> **Who both killed the Lord Jesus, and their own prophets, and have persecuted us; and they please not God, and are contrary to all men:**
>
> **Forbidding us to speak to the Gentiles that they might be saved, to fill up their sins alway: for the wrath is come upon them to the uttermost [1 Thess. 2:15–16].**

This I consider to be a remarkable passage of Scripture. It reveals a great principle: God permits sin to run its full course. The figure of speech which the prophets used was that the cup of iniquity must be filled up. God is permitting the cup to be filled. God won't check it so that Satan will never be able to say, "See, I never was given a chance because God wouldn't permit me to go all the way." I think the time of the Great Tribulation is the time when God will allow Satan full rein.

REWARD OF A TRUE WITNESS FOR CHRIST

But we, brethren, being taken from you for a short time in presence, not in heart, endeavoured the more abundantly to see your face with great desire [1 Thess. 2:17].

"Brethren"—again, this is the real brotherhood. This is the real ecumenical movement. When a person is in Christ Jesus, he is a brother to all others who are in Christ. Outside of Christ there is only the brotherhood of sinners.

"Being taken from you for a short time in presence, not in heart." Isn't this lovely of the apostle Paul? He was actually run out of Thessalonica, but his heart was still there. He hated to leave these Christians and wanted to be able to see them again. By the way, he did.

Wherefore we would have come unto you, even I Paul, once and again; but Satan hindered us [1 Thess. 2:18].

Paul had spiritual discernment to see that it was Satan's strategy that kept him from going to Thessalonica. The word *Satan* actually means "adversary."

I believe that today Satan seeks to hinder any program of getting out the Word of God. We have seen several instances of this. Many times my Bible teaching program has been on a radio station by which we were reaching an entire area, and things were going so nicely. Then a godless man would buy the station, and he would take all religious programs off the air. He doesn't want the Word of God to be given out.

For what is our hope, or joy, or crown of rejoicing? Are not even ye in the presence of our Lord Jesus Christ at his coming?

For ye are our glory and joy [1 Thess. 2:19–20].

Paul says that one of the great things he anticipates when Christ comes to take His church will be the opportunity to see these people whom he has led to the Lord. The Thessalonian believers whom he had won to Christ were a joy for him here and would be hereafter.

By the way, is anyone going to be in heaven who will come up to you and thank you for having a part in giving out the Word of God? Have you given your support to missions? If you have, someone you have never known, someone from the other side of the earth, may come up to you and thank you for your support of missions. He will thank you for being interested in getting out the Word of God because the Word reached him and enabled him to be saved. That, my friend, is going to be part of the reward that we will get in heaven. We need to recognize that. It is a wonderful hope to look forward to the time when Christ Jesus takes the church out of this world. It is even more joyous to know that someone who trusted Christ because of your witness will go along with you to meet the Lord!

CHAPTER 3

THEME: *The coming of Christ is a purifying hope*

The great theme of 1 Thessalonians is the rapture of the church. The great theme of 2 Thessalonians is the revelation of Christ; that is, His coming to the earth to establish His Kingdom. The thing that impresses me is the practicality of these doctrines which Paul taught to the Thessalonians. Today the schools of eschatology, or prophecy, have gotten this teaching way out into left field where it becomes sort of an extraneous thing. It becomes something that is nice to talk about and even to argue about, but it is not too meaningful to life. They do not teach it as something that must be geared into life and that can walk in shoe leather down here. Paul's teaching is entirely different.

The theme of this chapter is that the coming of Christ is a purifying hope. It will change your life, affect your life-style, if you hold to the hope of the rapture of the church; that is, the imminent coming of Christ for His own. If that doesn't affect your life, you don't really believe it. It is just sort of a theory or a philosophy with you. This theme becomes the very heart of the epistle, and we will be dealing with it from chapter 3 through verse 12 of chapter 4.

TIMOTHY BRINGS A GOOD REPORT OF THE THESSALONIANS

Wherefore when we could no longer forbear, we thought it good to be left at Athens alone [1 Thess. 3:1].

Paul longs to return to the Thessalonians but remains back at Athens alone so that he could send Timothy, and perhaps Silas, Dr. Luke, and others to Thessalonica.

Wherefore—this important word ties this chapter back in with what Paul had talked about in the previous chapter: the family relationship that exists in the church. He had been a mother to the church, a father to them, and a brother. He had led them to the Lord, and he loved them. He said that they would be his glory and his joy at the coming (parousia) of Christ, at the appearance of the Lord Jesus when all believers will receive their rewards.

Now because Paul had a real affection for them, he was frustrated in not being able to return to them. He had been hindered by Satan. Paul had to leave Thessalonica so quickly that there were many unfinished teachings and doctrines that he had not been able to develop fully. He not only longed to return, but he wondered about the future of the believers there. Paul desired to comfort them. In other words, he was demonstrating the thing he mentioned at the beginning of the letter—a labor of love.

Love is not affection or just a nice, comfortable, warm feeling around your heart. Love seeks the welfare of another. That is the way love is expressed for anyone. If you love someone, you seek his welfare and you actually would jeopardize your own life for the person whom you love.

> **And sent Timotheus, our brother, and minister of God, and our fellowlabourer in the gospel of Christ, to establish you, and to comfort you concerning your faith [1 Thess. 3:2].**

Because of his concern, Paul sent Timothy back to the Thessalonians. He calls Timothy "our brother, and minister of God." The word for "minister" is the Greek diakonos from which we get our English word deacon; it literally means "servant."

"Our fellowlabourer in the gospel of Christ." The gospel of Christ is the sphere of service. Paul was not just a do-gooder. Sometimes fundamentalists are criticized because our main objective is to get out the Word of God. We make that primary. We are criticized for not emphasizing the social aspect of the gospel enough. May I say that there has never been any great social movement that was not anchored in the preaching of the gospel. The child labor laws came out of the great Wesley meetings. The labor movement today owes a great deal to John

Wesley even though they have moved so far from the source that they don't recognize it. Hospitals have followed the preaching of the Word of God. If people will respond to the message of the gospel of Christ, their lives will be transformed, and then these good works will flow out of that change.

We are moving more and more into a welfare program in our country. This has become one of the most corrupt things that has ever taken place in our government. I don't think any of us can grasp the corruption that is connected with this vast program. Why does that happen? Because it is not anchored in the gospel of Christ.

The liberals who do the criticizing of us act as if they are the do-gooders. Have you ever known a do-gooder who really did something good? What *are* they doing? They actually encourage immorality and license. They haven't lifted up mankind. They are not able to release the kids from drugs. In fact, when I was in Portland, Oregon, one of the liberal churches there was using the church as a place to dispense birth control pills to the girls who wanted them!

Paul says that Timothy was a servant and that his sphere of service was the gospel of Christ. That is to be our sphere also. And when the gospel of Christ is given out, my friend, there will be a whole lot of doing good that will take place. The only criticism I've ever had of the do-gooders is that their doing good is merely temporary assistance. They are not helping folk permanently by bringing them into a right relationship with God. Only the gospel of Christ can do that.

"To *establish* you . . . concerning your faith." This same wonderful word was used back in the Book of Exodus when Moses went up to the mountain to hold up his hands in prayer to assure Israel's victory: "But Moses' hands were heavy; and they took a stone, and put it under him, and he sat thereon; and Aaron and Hur *stayed* up his hands, the one on the one side, and the other on the other side; and his hands were steady until the going down of the sun" (Exod. 17:12, italics mine). "Stayed up" is the same word as "establish." Paul sent Timothy over to them to stay them up, to hold them up, to establish them. People still need the same thing today. They need to be established in the faith.

"To comfort you concerning your faith." *Comfort* means "to encourage." He sent Timothy to hold the Thessalonians up and to encourage them in the faith.

> **That no man should be moved by these afflictions: for yourselves know that we are appointed thereunto [1 Thess. 3:3].**

Here is a statement that is a little hard for any of us to swallow. He says that "no man should be moved," which means he should not be disturbed, "by these afflictions." *Afflictions* here means "pressures, tensions."

Then Paul makes the amazing statement that "we are appointed thereunto." We know that we are going to go through storms. They will be temporary storms, but we cannot escape them. We are going to have trouble down here. The Word of God makes that very clear. Paul wants the Thessalonians to stand for the Lord in the midst of afflictions.

There are other passages of Scripture which teach this same truth. The Lord Jesus said, "These things I have spoken unto you, that in me ye might have peace. In the world ye shall have tribulation: but be of good cheer; I have overcome the world" (John 16:33). *Tribulation* is the trouble that all of us are going to have. There is no way around it. Yet the Lord Himself tells us to be of good cheer even in the midst of trouble.

If you are a believer, you are not going to escape trouble. To accept Christ does not mean to take out an insurance policy against suffering. The fact of the matter is that you *will* have trouble after you become a child of God, even if you haven't had any trouble before. He has never promised that we would miss the storm, but we will go through all the storms of life. What He does say very definitely and dogmatically is that He will go with us through the storms and that we will reach the harbor. Any boat which He is in will not go to the bottom of the Sea of Galilee but will reach the other side. You and I are in the process of going to the other side.

Paul reinforces this: "Yea, and all that will live godly in Christ

Jesus *shall suffer persecution*" (2 Tim. 3:12, italics mine). There are no "ifs," "ands," or "buts" about it (see 1 Pet. 4:12–19).

The time to be concerned is when there is no cloud in the sky, no ripple on the sea, and everything is smooth and nice. Then you might question your salvation. But if you are experiencing trouble down here, if the pressures and tensions of life are on you, then that is a sign that you are a child of God. This is the way God teaches us to rely on Him.

For verily, when we were with you, we told you before that we should suffer tribulation; even as it came to pass, and ye know [1 Thess. 3:4].

I remember hearing about a black congregation in Memphis, Tennessee, where the pastor asked for some favorite verses of Scripture. One man got up and said his favorite verse was, "And it came to pass." He sat down, and everyone looked puzzled. The pastor asked him how in the world that could be his favorite passage. He answered, "When I get in trouble, I turn to where it says, 'It came to pass,' and I know my troubles came to *pass*. They didn't come to stay." God will bring us through the storms. We will finally be rid of all our troubles. How wonderful that is. Our brother may have misapplied the verse, but his theology was absolutely accurate and agrees with what Paul is saying here.

Tribulation is the same word as *affliction*. This does not refer to the Great Tribulation. It refers to the "little tribulations." We are all going to have a little trouble down here. Such troubles are for the purpose of bringing us closer to God. They promote sanctification in the life of the believer.

For this cause, when I could no longer forbear, I sent to know your faith, lest by some means the tempter have tempted you, and our labour be in vain [1 Thess. 3:5].

"The tempter" is none other than Satan. In chapter 2 Paul said, "Satan hindered us." In other words, Paul is saying to the Thessalonians, "Satan is giving me a bad time, and I fear he may be giving you a bad time also."

Another purpose of afflictions is to test the genuineness of our belief. *Trouble* is the acid that tests the genuineness of the coin of belief. There are true believers and there are a lot of counterfeit ones. One thing that will really reveal the genuineness of faith is the ability to endure trouble through faith in God. Afflictions reveal the genuine believer, and this is the occasion of Paul's rejoicing.

> **But now when Timotheus came from you unto us, and brought us good tidings of your faith and charity, and that ye have good remembrance of us always, desiring greatly to see us, as we also to see you [1 Thess. 3:6].**

It was wonderful when Paul got word from them, and that word was a good report. They were enduring their afflictions.

> **Therefore, brethren, we were comforted over you in all our affliction and distress by your faith [1 Thess. 3:7].**

"In all our affliction"—Paul tells them that he has also had afflictions. The good report from them is a comfort to him.

> **For now we live, if ye stand fast in the Lord [1 Thess. 3:8].**

"We live" means that as believers we enjoy life. *If* should really be translated "since"—"since ye stand fast in the Lord." Even in trouble you can enjoy it—that's not always easy to do, my friend. This is what Peter writes: "Beloved, think it not strange concerning the fiery trial which is to try you, as though some strange thing happened unto you: But rejoice, inasmuch as ye are partakers of Christ's sufferings; that, when his glory shall be revealed, ye may be glad also with exceeding joy" (1 Pet. 4:12–13). You cannot lose as a Christian. Even if you have trouble, it is going to work out for your good—you can always be sure of that.

PAUL URGES CONTINUING GROWTH

For what thanks can we render to God again for you, for all the joy wherewith we joy for your sakes before our God [1 Thess. 3:9].

Joy is associated with life, and sorrow is associated with death. However, sorrow increases the capacity of the heart for joy. Paul wants the Thessalonians to know how to rejoice. Being a Christian is a wonderful thing!

Night and day praying exceedingly that we might see your face, and might perfect that which is lacking in your faith? [1 Thess. 3:10].

Paul's labor in Thessalonica was very rudely interrupted—he was run out of town—and he wanted to return to continue his teaching ministry. Paul *wanted* to teach the Word of God.

Now God himself and our Father, and our Lord Jesus Christ, direct our way unto you [1 Thess. 3:11].

Oh, how Paul prayed for the opportunity to return to them!

And the Lord make you to increase and abound in love one toward another, and toward all men, even as we do toward you:

To the end he may stablish your hearts unblameable in holiness before God, even our Father, at the coming of our Lord Jesus Christ with all his saints [1 Thess. 3:12–13].

"Abound in love." *Abound* means "exceed," and *love* is the Greek *agape*. In this epistle, love is seen only in action—"labor of love." It is not affection, but an active seeking of the welfare of another.

"To the end"—love has a purpose; it is not an end in itself.

"He may stablish your hearts unblameable in holiness"—the desired end of their love for one another is that they would develop a character of holiness. If you were tried in court for being a Christian, would there be enough evidence to convict you? We are going to appear before Him someday, and He is going to judge our works. This may terrify you, but He also is going to judge our character as believers and determine the reward we will receive. My Christian friend, what kind of a life are you living today?

"At the coming of our Lord Jesus Christ with all his saints." Most schools of thought would agree that this verse indicates that the saints are going to come with Christ when He comes to the earth to establish His Kingdom. But this verse also seems to indicate that He doesn't reward them until that time when He comes to the earth to establish His Kingdom. Yet many of us believe that believers will come before the judgment seat of Christ *before* that; that is, we believe that when He takes the church out of the world, the world enters the Great Tribulation period, and then he comes to establish His Kingdom at the end of the Great Tribulation period. So the question naturally arises: When is He going to present us "unblameable in holiness before God"? Is it when He takes the church out of the world? Or, will it be at the time He comes to the earth to establish His Kingdom? The answer depends upon our understanding of this phrase, "at the coming of our Lord Jesus Christ with all his saints."

There are different Greek words for "coming" or "appearing." The first of these words is *epiphaneia*; we get our word *epiphany* from it. The first coming of Christ was an epiphany. It has the idea of a shining through. The King James translation uses the word *appeared*: "For the grace of God that bringeth salvation hath appeared to all men" (Titus 2:11). The Lord Jesus came in person as a little Babe in Bethlehem more than nineteen hundred years ago. It was a breaking through, a shining through of the Lord. It was His epiphany. This word can be used of His first coming or His coming to take the church out of the world or His coming to set up His Kingdom. All three have the idea of a breaking through, a shining through, and the actual presence of the Lord Jesus.

A second Greek word is *apokalupsis*, which means a "revelation" or an "unveiling." That is actually the name of the Book of Revelation. One could hardly call His first coming an unveiling, because actually His glory was veiled in human flesh when He was born in Bethlehem. It was like the *shekinah* glory in the tabernacle of the Old Testament which was back in the Holy of Holies where only the high priest was allowed to enter. There was a veil which separated the Holy of Holies from the rest of the tabernacle. When the Lord Jesus was here the first time, His glory did not show forth; it was veiled in human flesh. When He comes again, His glory will shine forth. So this is a word that refers to His second coming.

The third Greek word is *parousia*. It literally means "presence" or "being alongside." It is commonly translated "coming," but it actually means "presence." We use *coming* in that same way today. I have been introduced to an audience with the words, "We are thankful for the coming of Dr. McGee." I wasn't coming at that time: I was already there. It means that I was present, sitting on the platform, and they were happy that I had come. Sometimes in the King James translation, *parousia* is translated as "presence" and sometimes as "coming." "Wherefore, my beloved, as ye have always obeyed, not as in my presence only . . ." (Phil. 2:12). In 1 Thessalonians 2:19 as well as in the verse we are considering, *parousia* is translated "coming."

Therefore, "at the coming of our Lord Jesus" refers to the fact that believers are going to be *present* with the Lord Jesus at the very moment that we are caught up to meet the Lord in the air. He will take us home to glory, to the place that He has prepared for us. So that this "coming" does not refer to the return of the Lord with His saints to establish His Kingdom, but to our coming to heaven into the presence of the Father. We have the same thought in 1 Thessalonians 2:19: "For what is our hope, or joy, or crown of rejoicing? Are not even ye in the presence of our Lord Jesus Christ at his coming?" We will come into the presence of the Lord Jesus and at that time will be presented "unblameable in holiness before God."

CHAPTER 4

THEME: The coming of Christ is a purifying hope; the coming of Christ is a comforting hope

HOW BELIEVERS ARE TO WALK

Furthermore then we beseech you, brethren, and exhort you by the Lord Jesus, that as ye have received of us how ye ought to walk and to please God, so ye would abound more and more [1 Thess. 4:1].

This section teaches how the believers are to walk down here in light of the coming of Christ. It is bound up in that little word *walk,* which we find in this verse and again in the twelfth verse. This is the practical aspect of the hope of the coming of the Lord. We like to look forward to the day when we shall be caught up to meet the Lord in the air. But, my friend, in the meantime our feet are down here on the ground and we need to do some walking. We are to walk in a way that will please God.

"As ye have received of us how ye ought to walk and to please God, so ye would abound more and more." We should keep improving. We should *grow* in grace and in the knowledge of Him. The walk of the believer is very important. It is emphasized in many portions of Scripture, and it is the emphasis here. A believer cannot do as he pleases; he does as Christ pleases.

For ye know what commandments we gave you by the Lord Jesus [1 Thess. 4:2].

In regard to their walk, we will find Paul giving some commandments to the Thessalonians. You will remember that the Lord Jesus also gave commandments. Some of these commandments are new commandments.

Let me say this very carefully: The Ten Commandments have no part in a sinner's salvation, nor are they standard for Christian conduct. The purpose of the Ten Commandments is to take us by the hand, as a pedagogue would take a little child by the hand, to bring us to the Cross and say to us, "Little fellow, you need a Savior!" The Ten Commandments are like a mirror which lets us see that we are sinners. The Ten Commandments were not given to save us; they were given to show us that we are sinners and that we need a Savior. That is their purpose.

However, there are commandments for believers, and the standard for Christian conduct which they set is on a much higher plane than the Ten Commandments. In chapter 5 we will find twenty-two commandments for believers given.

Now the question naturally arises: If man could not keep the Ten Commandments, how can he keep higher commandments? The Bible makes it very clear that man was not able to keep the Ten Commandments. The nation Israel transgressed these commandments as Simon Peter confessed: "And when there had been much disputing, Peter rose up, and said unto them, Men and brethren, ye know how that a good while ago God made choice among us, that the Gentiles by my mouth should hear the word of the gospel, and believe. . . . Now therefore why tempt ye God, to put a yoke upon the neck of the disciples, which neither our fathers nor we were able to bear? But we believe that through the grace of the Lord Jesus Christ we shall be saved, even as they" (Acts 15:7, 10–11).

Now if we can't keep the Ten Commandments, how are we to keep any higher commandments of Christian conduct? Man cannot do it himself. This can be attained only by the power of the Holy Spirit who dwells within the believer (see v. 8).

"For ye know what commandments we gave you by the Lord Jesus." Paul has some commandments for believers. We are not lawless. We should be disciplined, and we should be in obedience to Christ. It should be a love relationship—we should be motivated by love—the Lord Jesus said, "If ye love me, keep my commandments" (John 14:15).

For this is the will of God, even your sanctification, that ye should abstain from fornication [1 Thess. 4:3].

Sanctification is a very wonderful word, but I am afraid that it is greatly misunderstood. If you go through the Scriptures, you will find that sanctification has several different meanings. When it is used in reference to Christ, as it is here, it means that He has been made over to us sanctification—and you cannot improve on that! Therefore, it does not simply refer to a sinless state, but rather that we have been set apart for God. For example, Simon Peter speaks of the fact that ". . . holy men of God spake as they were moved by the Holy Ghost" (2 Pet. 1:21). Now some of those holy men have life stories that don't make them sound very holy! Moses, for instance, was a murderer. David, who wrote so many wonderful psalms, was also a murderer. But they were sanctified, holy, because they had been set aside for God.

Sanctification of the believer is a work of the Spirit of God. We need to review the threefold aspect of it, because this is so very important:

Positional sanctification means that Christ has been made unto us sanctification. We are accepted in the Beloved, and we will never be more saved than at the moment we put our trust in Christ. We are never accepted because of who we are, but because of what Christ has done. This positional sanctification is perfection in Christ.

Practical sanctification is the Holy Spirit working in our lives to produce a holiness in our walk. This practical sanctification will never be perfect so long as we are in these bodies with our old sinful flesh.

Total sanctification will occur in the future when we are conformed to the image of Christ Jesus. Then both the position *and* the practice of sanctification will be perfect.

The literal meaning of the word *sanctification* is to be "set apart for God." The moment a lost sinner comes to Christ and accepts Christ as Savior, that person is set aside for God's use. This is clearly taught in the Old Testament in the tabernacle. God taught the Old Testament believers great doctrinal truths through very simple, practical lessons. In the tabernacle there were vessels and instruments which were used in the sacrifices. After they had gone through the wilderness for forty years, those pots and pans and forks and spoons were pretty well beaten and battered. I don't think they were very attractive. I think that any good housewife would have said, "Let's trade them in on a new set. Let's throw these away." However, God called them *holy* vessels. They were holy because they were set aside for the use of God. That is what made them holy.

In the same way this applies to a person. When he comes to Christ, he is saved. He is redeemed; he belongs to Christ. Paul says, "This is the will of God, even your sanctification." You have been set aside for a holy purpose, for God's use. Every child of God—not just preachers or missionaries or Christian workers, but every believer—is set aside for the use of God.

"That ye should abstain from fornication." Don't think it was only the Thessalonians who needed this admonition from Paul. Don't think they were the only ones who engaged in sins, especially the sins of the flesh. Don't think it was only in Roman times that idolatry involved sins of sex. Today we are seeing the rise of the worship of Satan and the practice of the occult. There are all kinds of amulets and rituals connected with such worship. Also there is astrology which seeks to tell people about themselves. And there is always sex involved in all of it.

The great tragedy today is to hear of some Christian worker who has become involved in sexual sin. And, unfortunately, there are even churches that will defend a minister who has been guilty of such. We are people who are supposed to be set aside for the use of God! Paul says that you cannot be involved in sexual sin and at the same time be used of God. One cannot live in sin and be a preacher or singer or Sunday school teacher or an officer in the church. I don't care who you are, if you do, you will wreck the work of God.

Now, should a Christian strive for holiness? I think so. But you and I need to recognize that it is only in Christ that we can be acceptable to God. Paul says that we have been sanctified, brought to this high state, set apart for the use of God. Now what?—

> That every one of you should know how to possess his
> vessel in sanctification and honour;
>
> Not in the lust of concupiscence, even as the Gentiles
> which know not God [1 Thess. 4:4-5].

All around these Thessalonian believers were the pagans who combined sex and religion. Sex was a religion among the Greeks. You could go to Corinth and find that out, but you didn't have to go to Corinth—you could find it out right in Thessalonica.

Paul says that we are to live a life that commends the gospel. The loose living that we find among some believers today brings the gospel into disrepute. Such people are not living for God or serving God. You cannot serve God and live in sin. He doesn't accept that.

"That every one of you should know how to possess his vessel in sanctification and honour." The immorality that exists in our day is absolutely astounding. A very fine Christian leader who holds Bible classes on the campus of a college here in California told me that the boys' dormitory is Sodom and the girls' dormitory is Gomorrah. These poor kids know all about sex, but they don't know about love. God says that the body should be saved for the marriage relationship, and this applies to men and women. There are all sorts of reasons given for the fact that there is so much unhappiness in marriage. The problem is that the marriage partners are not people who have been set apart for the use of God and who are faithful to each other in a love relationship. When a person saves his body for marriage and is faithful to his partner, he is possessing his vessel "in sanctification and honour." Such should be the practice of every child of God. Believe me, Paul puts it on the line.

> That no man go beyond and defraud his brother in any
> matter: because that the Lord is the avenger of all such,
> as we also have forewarned you and testified [1 Thess.
> 4:6].

"That no man go beyond and defraud his brother in any matter." You have to be honest if you are going to be a child of God.

"Because that the Lord is the avenger of all such." I've lived long enough as a Christian and as a pastor to see this principle worked out in the lives of many believers. I've observed certain believers who have been dishonest in their dealings with others, and God *is* an avenger—He moves in and judges them.

For God hath not called us unto uncleanness, but unto holiness [1 Thess. 4:7].

A child of God cannot continue in sin. The Prodigal Son may get in the pigpen for a time, but he won't *live* in the pigpen.

He therefore that despiseth, despiseth not man, but God, who hath also given unto us his holy Spirit [1 Thess. 4:8].

A child of God is indwelt by the Holy Spirit. He cannot continue to live in sin because the Holy Spirit is the *Holy* Spirit. The time will come when the child of God will long for holiness in his own life.

The Holy Spirit is the only means by which we can live for God. We see in Paul's Galatian epistle that the child of God is not to indulge in the sins of the flesh. Instead, there should be the manifestation of the fruit of the Spirit in the life. In Romans 8:3, Paul makes it very clear: "For what the law could not do. . . ." Why? Is the Law wrong? No, the Law is not wrong; the Ten Commandments are not wrong. The problem is with man, not with the Law. Man cannot attain to the level of the Ten Commandments, nor can he live by the commandments in the New Testament. It is the Holy Spirit within the believer who has been given to him to enable him to live a life for God.

God has given the Holy Spirit to *every* believer. He is not something to be sought after a person is saved. The moment a sinner trusts Christ, that person is indwelt by the Spirit of God. In Acts 19 we find that when Paul arrived in Ephesus, he found people who were professing to be Christians, but he saw that they were not indwelt by the Spirit of God. He asked them whether they had received the Holy

Spirit when they were saved. They told him they had never even heard about such things; they had heard only of the baptism of John. So Paul preached the gospel to them, and then they were saved and received the Holy Spirit. You receive the Holy Spirit only when you are converted and come to Christ. At that point the believer receives and is baptized with the Holy Spirit and is placed into the body of believers to function in it. A person may have many infillings of the Spirit after that, and I think we need a constant infilling of the Holy Spirit. It is only the indwelling Holy Spirit that enables us to lead holy lives.

> **But as touching brotherly love ye need not that I write unto you: for ye yourselves are taught of God to love one another [1 Thess. 4:9].**

Love is the subject, and the statement he makes is rather amazing. A believer must have love for the brethren. It is a supernatural love that is taught of God: "The fruit of the Spirit is love." It is not a theoretical kind of love, not just an abstract term. We have mentioned before that it cannot be just love in the abstract, but it must be love in the concrete. Such love can only be produced in the hearts of believers by the Holy Spirit. Notice that after Paul speaks of the Holy Spirit, brotherly love is the first thing that he mentions.

He writes, "As touching brotherly love ye need not that I write unto you: for ye yourselves are taught of God to love one another." I believe that love is the identifying mark of a child of God.

My roommate in college and I could wrestle, fight, argue, try to get dates with the same girl, and all that sort of thing. One day we really had had a knock-down-drag-out fight. We had literally torn up the room. He proceeded to tell me what he thought of me, and it was not very complimentary. Then I proceeded to tell him what I thought of him and that wasn't very complimentary either. All of a sudden it occurred to me, "Look, you are the greatest proof that I am a child of God! One of the evidences that a person is a child of God is that he loves his brother. John emphasizes it and it is in 1 Thessalonians that we are taught of God to love our brother. In spite of the fact that you are the most contemptible person I have ever met, the most unlovely person I have ever met, I love you!" He looked startled and began to laugh. "You know, I love you, and you're lots worse than I am!"

This man is now a retired preacher, just as I am. Once in a while we have an opportunity to see one another. He is still a very ornery individual, but I love him because he is a child of God. And I think he loves me. That is the proof that we are the children of God.

> **And indeed ye do it toward all the brethren which are in all Macedonia: but we beseech you, brethren, that ye increase more and more [1 Thess. 4:10].**

Love for the brethren is an area for growth and development. Very candidly, some of the saints are not very lovely. Someone has put that fact into this little jingle:

> To dwell above with saints in love
> Oh, that will be glory.
> But to stay below with the saints I know—
> Well, that's another story.

These Thessalonians did love the brethren, but evidently their love had not reached the *summum bonum* of life. They weren't perfect in their love, and there was still room for improvement.

There are going to be some personality conflicts among the saints. It may be better for such people not to be together too much nor to put arms around each other and walk together. That doesn't mean we should hate them. We can still love them as the children of God. For example, I know a minister whose methods I absolutely despise, but I can truthfully say that I love him. I know of no one who gets up and presents Jesus Christ as wonderfully as this man does, and I love him for it.

The real test is our love for the brethren. If you want to put the blue litmus paper down in your life to test it and find out whether or not you are a genuine believer, this is the place to put it down: Do you love the brethren?

And that ye study to be quiet, and to do your own business, and to work with your own hands, as we commanded you [1 Thess. 4:11].

"That ye study to be quiet." That is an interesting commandment for Christians. We have all kinds of schools today to teach people to speak. Every seminary has a public speaking class. Perhaps they should also have a class that would teach their students to be quiet. A lot of saints need such a course!

A lady went to a "tongues meeting," and the leader thought she was interested in speaking in tongues. He asked her, "Madam, would you like to speak in tongues?" She answered, "No, I would like to lose about forty feet off the one I have now!" We need to study to be quiet. That is a commandment.

"And to do your own business"—that is another good commandment. It means to mind your own business. "Tend to your own knitting" is the way I used to hear it as a boy. Keep your nose out of the affairs of other people. This is good advice for Christians.

"And to work with your own hands, as we commanded you." I believe that every Christian should have some type of activity whereby he is doing something that is tangible for God. That would be a wonderful thing.

That ye may walk honestly toward them that are without, and that ye may have lack of nothing [1 Thess. 4:12].

"Walk honestly"—this is also something that the saints of God need to do today. It will gain the respect and the confidence of mankind. Our walk should be honest before God and man.

I have letters from several organizations which use methods to raise money that seem very questionable to me. Certain organizations have men out contacting people who have become senile, attempting to get them to make their wills over to their organizations. That is one reason you ought to make your will *before* you become senile. There are unscrupulous people who are out to get your money—there is no question about that. A child of God cannot do such questionable things because we are to "walk honestly toward them that are without." That means that all dealings with unbelievers are to be scrupulously honest. God will judge us if we do not walk honestly.

THE COMING OF CHRIST IS A COMFORTING HOPE

We come now to the next section of this epistle, a section which has been labeled one of the most important prophetic passages in the Scriptures. It teaches the imminent and impending coming of Christ for His church. That does not mean the immediate or soon coming of Christ. Paul never uses an expression like that. He did not want people to assume it would be in their own lifetime or shortly afterward. It has been more than nineteen hundred years now. But when we say that the coming of Christ is imminent, we mean that it is approaching or that it is the next event on the agenda of God's program.

Let me illustrate my point. One time when Mrs. McGee and I flew to Florida on a new DC-10 from the Los Angeles International Airport, we had a friendly captain who began to talk to us soon after our flight had begun: "The weather is lovely here in Southern California as you can see. The weather in Miami, Florida, is also very good, and we expect it to be nice when we arrive there. We fly over Texas, and of course nobody knows what the weather will be there, but we should have a good flight today. Our next stop is Miami." Now there was not a single passenger who jumped up, grabbed his luggage, and rushed for the door because the captain had said, "Our next stop is Miami." That stop was imminent. In other words, we would not make any other stop before that one. It would be five hours before we would arrive at Miami, but we were prepared for that stop because it was imminent—it was the next stop.

The difference between waiting for the stop at Miami and waiting for the coming of Christ for His church is that we knew that Miami was five hours away. We don't know how far away the coming of Christ is. It could be five hours or five days or five weeks or five months or five years or five hundred years. We simply do not know. Still, it is imminent; it is the next event.

Paul makes it very clear that he believed in the imminent return of Christ. In verse 15 of this chapter he says, "We which are alive and remain unto the coming of the Lord." Paul believed that the Lord Jesus *could* come in his lifetime. He did not say or believe that He *would* come in his lifetime, but he said that He could come. This was the attitude he expressed as he wrote to Titus: "Looking for that blessed hope, and the glorious appearing of the great God and our Saviour Jesus Christ" (Titus 2:13).

There are those who accuse Paul of changing his position on the imminent coming of Christ as he himself grew older. Remember that this epistle to the Thessalonians was his earliest letter. Did Paul change his theology? When he wrote to the Philippians he was an old man, a prisoner in Rome, and he said: "For our conversation [citizenship] is in heaven; from whence also we look for the Saviour, the Lord Jesus Christ" (Phil. 3:20). Paul, at the end of his life, was still looking for Him. In other words, Christ's coming was imminent.

Paul labeled this coming of Christ for His church, when we are to be caught up to meet the Lord in the air, the *rapture* of the church. There are those today who hold a different viewpoint. They say the Bible does not teach the Rapture and that one cannot find that word in the New Testament. I insist that it is there. It is found in this chapter in verse 17: "Then we which are alive and remain shall be caught up together with them in the clouds, to meet the Lord in the air: and so shall we ever be with the Lord." The Greek word translated as "caught up" is *harpazō*. It means "to catch up or grasp hastily, to snatch up, to lift, to transport, or to rapture." *Rapture* is just as good a word as *caught up*. It is a matter of semantics, whichever word you choose to use. The fact is that the Bible teaches that believers in Christ are to be caught up in the clouds to meet the Lord in the air. Paul taught the rapture of the church. Now if you would like, you could say you believe in the *harpazō*—that's the original Greek word, and it means "rapture" and it means "caught up." Nonetheless, the point is that the rapture of the church can take place at any moment; it is the next happening in the program of God.

Now I want to make a very startling statement about this passage of Scripture. Actually, the primary consideration here is not the Rapture.

The precise question Paul is answering is: What about believers who have died before the Rapture has taken place?

We need to review the background of this epistle in order to understand why this question was so important to the Thessalonian believers. Paul went to Thessalonica on his second missionary journey. ". . . three sabbath days [he] reasoned with them out of the scriptures" (Acts 17:2). That means that Paul was there less than a month. In that month's time, he performed a herculean task. He did the work of a missionary. He preached the gospel, converts were made, and he established a church. Then he taught these new believers the great truths of the Christian faith. It is interesting that he even taught them of the rapture of the church.

When I was a young preacher in a denomination, they didn't have much to say about prophecy. Very candidly, I don't think the ministers knew very much about it. They would give an excuse, saying, "You shouldn't preach on that. That is deep truth and should be given to mature saints. It shouldn't be given to new believers." Well, it's too bad that Paul didn't know that, because he hadn't been with the Thessalonians for a complete month and yet he was teaching them prophecy. In fact, when we get to the second epistle we will find that he taught them about the Great Tribulation and the Man of Sin, the Antichrist who is to come. Paul ran the whole gamut of prophecy for these Thessalonians. It is nonsense to say this is not to be given to new believers. It is to be taught to them, and Paul is the demonstration of that.

It is clear that Paul taught the Thessalonians that the rapture of the church might occur at any moment, that it was imminent. Then Paul left Thessalonica; he went to Berea, established a church and was there for some time. Then he took a ship and went over to Athens. We don't know how long he was there either. He was waiting for Timothy and Silas to bring word from Thessalonica. They didn't come, and he went on down to Corinth. After he was there for awhile, Timothy and Silas came. They came with questions from the Thessalonians to ask of Paul. So Paul wrote 1 Thessalonians to encourage them and to answer their specific questions with regard to the rapture of the church. During this unknown interval of time after Paul had left them, some of the saints in Thessalonica had died. A question arose in the minds of the believers. *Had they missed the Rapture?*

Obviously Paul had taught them the imminent coming of Christ, or this question would not be pertinent at all. Paul had told them that the Lord Jesus might come at any moment. These saints had died, and the Lord hadn't come—had they missed the Rapture? What would happen to them? Paul gives the answer to this question in this epistle.

To us the question the Thessalonians had is not meaningful in the same way as it was to them. That is because you and I live nineteen hundred years this side of 1 Thessalonians, and literally millions of believers have already gone down through the doorway of death. Therefore, most of the church has already gone ahead, and a small minority remains in the world.

Paul had taught the Thessalonians that the coming of Christ was imminent, and this is still what we believe today. Between where we are right this moment and the coming of Christ for the church it is tissue-thin, which means it could happen any moment—even before you finish reading this page—or the coming of Christ could be way down yonder in the future.

There is a grave danger today in setting dates for the coming of the Lord. Some are doing that, and it is dangerous because they do not know when He will return. The Lord said that we do not know the hour He will come. They might pick the year correctly, but they surely won't pick the hour—I don't think they will even hit the year. When they set dates, they are robbing believers of the opportunity of looking for Him to come.

Now the Thessalonians were concerned about the saints who had died before the Rapture had taken place. We need to keep that in mind as we go through the rest of this chapter.

> **But I would not have you to be ignorant, brethren, concerning them which are asleep, that ye sorrow not, even as others which have no hope [1 Thess. 4:13].**

"I would not have you to be ignorant." I love the way Paul says that. We have seen it before in the Corinthian epistles. When Paul says, "I would not have you ignorant, brethren," you can pretty well put it down that the brethren are ignorant. Paul just didn't come out and say so in a flat-footed and crude way. He is more polite and diplomatic. I would say that he did it in a very Christian way.

"Concerning them which are asleep." Paul is referring to the death of the body. This never refers to the soul or the spirit of man, because the spirit of man does not die. We shall note that as we move through this section, but first I want to mention several reasons that the death of the body is spoken of as being "asleep."

1. There is a similarity between sleep and death. A dead body and a sleeping body are actually very similar. I'm sure you have been to a funeral where someone has remarked that So-and-so looks just as if he were asleep. Well, in a way it is true—the body of a believer is asleep. A sleeper does not cease to exist, and the inference is that the dead do not cease to exist just because the body is asleep. Sleep is temporary; death is also temporary. Sleep has its waking; death has its resurrection. It is not that life is existence and death is non-existence, you see.

2. The word which is translated "asleep" has its root in the Greek word *keimai*, which means "to lie down." And the very interesting thing is that the word for "resurrection" is a word that refers only to the body. It is *anastasis*, and it comes from two Greek words: *histemi* which means "to stand," and *ana*, the preposition, "up." It is only the body which can stand up in resurrection.

C. S. Lewis in his *Screwtape Letters* uses a little sarcasm to ridicule the liberals who believe that the resurrection is a resurrection of the spirit and not of the body. He asks what position the soul or the spirit takes when it lies down in death, or what position the spirit takes when it stands up in resurrection! If you want to believe in soul sleep, you must explain how a soul can lie down and then stand up. Obviously "asleep" refers to the body.

The same Greek word for "sleep" is used here as is used when referring to a natural sleep when the body lies down in bed. Let me give you two illustrations of this. "And when he rose up from prayer, and was come to his disciples, he found them *sleeping* for sorrow" (Luke 22:45, italics mine). Imagine that Peter, James, and John went to sleep at this time of crisis! The word is the same word that is used here in 1 Thessalonians. Again, in Acts 12:6, "And when Herod would have brought him forth, the same night Peter was *sleeping* between two soldiers, bound with two chains: and the keepers before the door kept the prison" (italics mine). One thing we know for sure about Simon Peter is that he didn't have insomnia! Even at times of great crisis, he was able to sleep. Again, the same word for "sleep" is used, and it is the natural sleep of the body.

3. The Bible teaches that the body returns to the dust from which it was created, but the spirit returns to God who gave it. Even the Old Testament teaches this. In Ecclesiastes 12:7 we read: "Then shall the dust return to the earth as it was: and the spirit shall return unto God who gave it." "The dust"—that is our body. God told Adam, ". . . for dust thou art, and unto dust shall thou return" (Gen. 3:19). It was the body that was taken from the dust, and then God breathed into man the breath of life, or the spirit, you see. It is the body that will go to sleep until the resurrection—only the body. The spirit of a believer will return to God.

The spirit or the soul does not die, and therefore the spirit or the soul is not raised. Only the body can lie down in death, and only the body can stand up in resurrection. This is quite obvious when Paul says that to be absent from the body is to be present with the Lord (see 2 Cor. 5:8).

The body is merely a frail tent that is laid aside temporarily in death. "For we know that if our earthly house of this tabernacle were dissolved, we have a building of God, an house not made with hands, eternal in the heavens" (2 Cor. 5:1). The Greek word for "tabernacle" here is skenos, which means "a tent." The bodies we live in are tents. I have news for you: You may live in a home that cost $250,000, but the place where you really live is a little tent. God put every single one of us into a tent. It is not a matter of some living in a hovel and some in a mansion—we have all been given the same kind of tent. You could reduce the body to its component chemicals, and I am told the whole amount would sell for about $4.00, although inflated prices may push it a little higher. Everyone of us lives in a tent that is worth about

$4.00! It can be blown down at any moment. If you don't believe that, step in front of a car and you will find that your tent will fold up and silently slip away. Our bodies are actually very frail.

"For in this we groan, earnestly desiring to be clothed upon with our house which is from heaven" (2 Cor. 5:2). "For we that are in this tabernacle do groan . . ." (2 Cor. 5:4). We groan within our tents. Have you discovered that?

I met an old man at the corner bus stop many years ago. He must have been pretty close to eighty. He was swearing like a sailor. I said to him, "Brother, you won't be here very long, and you are going to have to answer to God."

"How do you know I won't be here very long?" he asked.

"God is telling you so. He has put gray in your hair, a totter in your step, a stoop in your shoulder, and a shortness of breath when you walk. He is trying to tell you that you won't be here much longer. You are living in a little tent down here, and you are going to be slipping away soon."

I am told that when President Adams was an old man, a friend inquired about his health. He answered that he was fine, but the house he lived in was getting rickety and was not in good repair. That is the kind of body each of us is living in, my friend.

When I was a young man, I could bound up and down the steps to my study. Today it is different. I come down the steps one at a time, and there is no more bounding. My knees hurt, and I groan. My wife tells me I groan too much, but I tell her it is scriptural to groan. Paul said that we groan in these bodies.

These old bodies are going to be put into the grave, and there they are going to sleep. The spirit goes to be with the Lord.

Paul wrote, "Therefore we are always confident, knowing that, whilst we are at home in the body, we are absent from the Lord: (For we walk by faith, not by sight:)" (2 Cor. 5:6-7). Now we are at home in this body; this is where we live. People don't really get to see us, you know—we are hidden in our bodies. Sometimes people who come to rallies or services when I speak, tell me they have heard me on the radio and they have come just to see how I look. I always feel like saying, "You really haven't seen me. All you have seen is a head and two hands sticking out of a suit of clothes. You don't see me—I live within this body." This house I live in isn't in such good repair, but that's where I will live as long as I walk on this earth.

Paul goes on to say, "We are confident, I say, and willing rather to be absent from the body, and to be present with the Lord" (2 Cor. 5:8). I can't think of anything lovelier than that. If you should attend my funeral, I wouldn't want you to come by and say that I look so natural. Friend, I won't even be there. You will just be looking at my tent that I have left behind. It's my old house, that has been put to sleep. I will be gone to be with the Lord. At the resurrection our bodies will be raised up.

Many years ago in the city of New York (in fact, it was way back in the day when liberalism was called modernism, back in the 1920s) they had an argument about whether resurrection was spiritual. The liberal even today claims it's spiritual. He doesn't believe in bodily resurrection at all. A very famous Greek scholar from the University of Chicago read a paper on the passage from 1 Corinthians 15: "It is sown a natural body; it is raised a spiritual body. There is a natural body, and there is a spiritual body" (1 Cor. 15:44). His paper put the emphasis on the word *spiritual*. He concluded by saying, "Now, brethren, you can see that resurrection is spiritual because it says it's spiritual." The liberals all applauded, and somebody made a motion that they print that manuscript and circulate it.

Well, a very fine conservative Greek scholar was there, and he stood up. When he stood, all the liberals were a little uneasy because he could ask very embarrassing questions. He said, "I'd like to ask the author of the paper a question." Very reluctantly, the good doctor stood up. "Now, doctor, which is stronger, a noun or an adjective? A very simple question, but I'd like for you to answer it." He could see the direction he was going and didn't want to answer it, but he had to say that a noun is stronger, of course. "Now doctor, I'm amazed that you presented the paper that you did today. You put the emphasis upon an adjective, and the strong word is the noun. Now, let's look at that again. 'It is sown a natural body; it is raised a spiritual *body*.'" He said, "The only thing that is carried over in resurrection is the body. It's one kind of body when it dies, a natural body. It's raised a body, but a spiritual body, dominated now by the spirit—but it's still a body." And they never did publish that paper. They decided it would be better not to publish it. May I say to you, just a simple little exercise in grammar would have answered this great professor's whole manuscript and his entire argument which he presented at that time.

Daniel is another writer who spoke of the death of the body as "sleep." "And many of them that sleep in the dust of the earth shall awake, some to everlasting life, and some to shame and everlasting contempt" (Dan. 12:2). Dust will go back to dust—that's the body; but the spirit goes to God who sent it.

4. The early Christians adopted a very wonderful word for the burying places of their loved ones—the Greek word *koimeterion*, which means "a rest house for strangers, a sleeping place." It is the same word from which we get our English word *cemetery*. The same word was used in that day for inns, or what we would call a hotel or motel. A Hilton Hotel, a Ramada Inn or a Holiday Inn—they are the places where you spend the night to sleep. You expect to get up the next day and continue your journey. This is the picture of the place where you bury your believing loved ones. You don't weep when you have a friend who goes and spends a weekend in a Hilton Hotel, do you? No, you rejoice with him. The body of the believer has just been put into a motel until the resurrection. One day the Lord is coming and that body is going to be raised up.

Now let us return to our consideration of the actual text of verse 13: "That ye sorrow not, even as others [the rest] which have no hope." The pagan world had no hope; so for them death was a frightful thing. In Thessalonica they have found an inscription that says: "After death no reviving, after the grave no meeting again." The Greek poet Theocritus wrote, "Hopes are among the living; the dead are without hope." That was the belief of the ancient world. It is pretty pessimistic and doleful.

Believers are not to sorrow as the pagans. I have officiated at many funeral services during the years of my ministry, and I can always tell if the family is Christian. I can tell by the way the people weep whether they have hope or not. Christians weep, of course—there is nothing wrong with that. Paul never says that believers are not to weep. What he does say is that we are not to sorrow as the others which have no hope. A Christian has a sorrow at the death of a loved one, but he also has hope.

> **For if we believe that Jesus died and rose again, even so them also which sleep in Jesus will God bring with him [1 Thess. 4:14].**

I want you to notice that Paul says that "Jesus *died* and rose again." It doesn't say Jesus slept—He *died*. How accurate this is!

There are three kinds of death in Scripture. There is *physical death*, which is the separation of the spirit from the body. That is what we ordinarily call death. Adam didn't actually die physically until 930 years after the Fall.

Then there is *spiritual death*. Paul says that to be carnally minded is death, which is separation from God. This is what happened to man in the Garden of Eden when God said that man would die in the day he ate of the fruit. Man became separated from God. Adam hid from God; he ran from God when God came into the garden—there was now a separation between them. Adam *did* die the day he ate the fruit—a spiritual death. Paul describes this spiritual death in Ephesians 2:1: "And you hath he quickened, who were dead in trespasses and sins."

A famous judge toured around this country some years ago giving a lecture entitled "Millions Now Living Will Never Die." There followed him a famous Baptist preacher whose lecture was "Millions Now Living Are Already Dead." And they *were* dead—spiritually dead.

The third death is *eternal death*. That is eternal separation from God. This is the second death described in Revelation 20:14.

> **For this we say unto you by the word of the Lord, that we which are alive and remain unto the coming of the Lord shall not prevent them which are asleep [1 Thess. 4:15].**

"By the word of the Lord" is Paul's assurance that he is giving God's answer to their question. Paul knows that they had been worrying

about those who had died before the Rapture and wants them to know
that the dead in Christ will have part in the Rapture.

"We which are alive and remain unto the coming of the Lord shall
not prevent them which are asleep." The word *prevent* is an old English word meaning "precede." Those who are alive at the time of the
Rapture will not be going ahead of them—in fact, the dead in Christ
will be going first.

> **For the Lord himself shall descend from heaven with a**
> **shout, with the voice of the archangel, and with the**
> **trump of God: and the dead in Christ shall rise first**
> **[1 Thess. 4:16].**

"The Lord himself shall descend from heaven." I love that—He won't
be sending angels. When He comes to the earth to establish His Kingdom, He will send His angels to the four corners of the earth to gather
the elect, who will be both Israelites and Gentiles who enter the Kingdom. However, there is no angel ministry connected with the rapture
of the church. Angels announced the birth of Christ, but how was He
announced? As the Son of David, the newborn King. He was announced as a King. The wise men wanted to know where they could
find Him who was born King of the Jews. In contrast to this, at the
establishment of the church on the Day of Pentecost, there were no
angels. The Holy Spirit Himself came down. When the Lord takes His
church out of the world, the Lord Himself shall descend from heaven.
There will be no angels. Angels are connected with Israel but not with
the church at all.

He will descend from heaven "with a shout." That is the voice of
command. It is the same voice which He used when He stood at the
tomb of Lazarus and said, "Lazarus, come forth" (see John 11:43).

"The voice of the archangel." Now wait, isn't that an angel connected with the Rapture? No, it is *His* voice that will be like the voice
of an archangel. It is the quality of His voice, the majesty and the
authority of it.

"The trump of God." Will there be trumpets there? No, it is *His* voice that will be like a trumpet. Can we be sure of this? In Revelation 1:10, John, who was exiled to the Isle of Patmos, wrote, "I was in the Spirit on the Lord's day, and heard behind me a great voice, as of a trumpet." He turned to see who it was, and he saw the glorified Christ. It is the voice of the glorified Christ that is like the sound of a trumpet.

That ought to get rid of all this foolishness about Gabriel blowing his horn or blowing a trumpet. I don't think Gabriel even owns a trumpet, but if he has one, he won't need to blow it. The Lord Jesus is not going to need the help of Gabriel. Do you think the Lord Jesus needed Gabriel to come and help Him raise Lazarus from the dead? Can you imagine the Lord Jesus at the tomb of Lazarus saying, "Gabriel, won't you come over here and help Me get this man out of the grave?" How absolutely foolish! The Lord Jesus will not need anyone to help Him. When He calls His church, their bodies will come up out of the graves.

> **Then we which are alive and remain shall be caught up together with them in the clouds, to meet the Lord in the air: and so shall we ever be with the Lord [1 Thess. 4:17].**

Again, "caught up" is the Greek *harpazō*, meaning "to grasp hastily, snatch up, to lift, transport, or rapture."

It is going to be a very orderly procedure. The dead will rise first. Here comes Stephen out of the grave. It may be that he will lead the procession since he was the first martyr. Then there will be the apostles and all those millions who have laid down their lives for Jesus. They will just keep coming from right down through the centuries. Finally, if we are alive at that time, we will bring up the rear of the parade. We will be way down at the tail end of it. Most of the church has already gone in through the doorway of death.

> **Wherefore comfort one another with these words [1 Thess. 4:18].**

Does he say, "Wherefore terrify one another with these words"? Of course not. My Bible says, "Wherefore *comfort* one another." It not only means to comfort in the usual sense of the word, but also to instruct and to exhort one another and to *talk* about these things. My friend, Jesus is going to take His own out of this world someday! What a glorious, wonderful comfort this is! The bodies of the dead will be lifted out. Then whoever is alive at that time will be caught up together with them to meet the Lord in the air. So shall we ever be with the Lord. In fact, we shall come back with Him to the earth to reign with Him at the time He sets up His Kingdom.

CHAPTER 5

THEME: The coming of Christ is a rousing hope

In this final chapter of 1 Thessalonians we see the Christian's *actions* in view of the return of Christ. In chapter 1, you will recall, we considered the Christian's *attitude* toward the return of Christ. Now, if the attitude does not lead to action, something is radically wrong. The coming of Christ is a rousing hope which leads to action!

CALL TO BE AWAKE AND ALERT IN VIEW OF CHRIST'S COMING

The believer in Christ is to be awake and alert in view of Christ's coming, because the believer will not enter into that awful night of the Great Tribulation period, which is labeled the *Day* of the Lord. That Day of the Lord begins with night because that is God's way of marking time. He begins that way in Genesis where it says that the evening and the morning were the first day. God begins in night but moves to light. So the Great Tribulation leads into the glorious millennial reign of Christ when the Sun of Righteousness will arise with healing in His wings.

The *Day of the Lord* is an expression we need to examine.

> **But of the times and the seasons, brethren, ye have no need that I write unto you [1 Thess. 5:1].**

"Times and seasons" are not the property of the church; they belong to this earth and to an earthly people—both Israel and the Gentiles who will be saved in that day. The church is looking for a Person, not for times and seasons. The word for "time" is the Greek *chronos*, from which we get our English word *chronology*. The times and seasons or the chronology is not for the church.

For yourselves know perfectly that the day of the Lord so cometh as a thief in the night [1 Thess. 5:2].

The Lord Jesus does not come to the church like a thief in the night. The church is looking for and waiting for the Lord to come. You don't wait for a thief and look for him and leave a note for him on the back door when you leave your house—"I left the back door open for you, Mr. Thief, and you'll find the family silver in the third drawer to the right in the dining room." I don't imagine you have ever left such a note. The chances are that you check everything before you leave the house, making sure that your home is doubly locked. You want to keep the thief out. So the Lord Jesus does not come as a thief to the church. However, the Lord Jesus does come like a thief to the world *after* the church has been raptured. As I have said, the Day of the Lord will come suddenly to the earth, and it will begin with the night of the Great Tribulation period; then finally Christ will come personally to this earth.

The Day of the Lord will come *suddenly*—

For when they shall say, Peace and safety; then sudden destruction cometh upon them, as travail upon a woman with child; and they shall not escape [1 Thess. 5:3].

Do you notice the change of pronouns here? In the first two verses Paul is addressing the "brethren," and he says that it is not necessary for him to write to them about the times and seasons, because they will have nothing to do with it—believers will be gone at that time. But here in verse 3 the pronoun changes to "they"—"when *they* shall say, Peace and safety."

Again let me repeat that the Day of the Lord is a period of time which begins with the Great Tribulation and goes through the millennial reign of Christ here upon the earth. There are many passages of Scripture which speak of this. For example, in Isaiah, chapters 12—13, you can read how God moves down in judgment on society and government, on the military and commerce and art and pomp and pride and religion. "Behold, the day of the LORD cometh, cruel both with wrath and fierce anger, to lay the land desolate: and he shall destroy the sinners thereof out of it" (Isa. 13:9). It starts out as a day of wrath: "For the stars of heaven and the constellations thereof shall not give their light: the sun shall be darkened in his going forth, and the moon shall not cause her light to shine" (Isa. 13:10). In the prophecy of Joel we are told: "Alas for the day! for the day of the LORD is at hand, and as a destruction from the Almighty shall it come" (Joel 1:15). Joel goes on in chapter 2 to describe it as "a day of darkness and of gloominess, a day of clouds and of thick darkness . . ." (Joel 2:2). That is the picture given to us in the Old Testament. The Day of the Lord is a period which begins with the Great Tribulation and goes through the millennial reign of Christ. That is a theme in the Old Testament.

Now the event described in chapter 4—the coming of Christ to take the church out of the world—is not even mentioned in the Old Testament. It is there by type, of course, such as the experiences of Enoch and Elijah, both of whom were taken up alive to be with the Lord. But it is not taught in the Old Testament that the Lord Jesus is going to take a company of people out of this earth to be with Himself. This is a glorious, wonderful truth which was revealed first in the Upper Room when the Lord Jesus said, ". . . I go to prepare a place for you. And if I go and prepare a plcae for you, I will come again, and receive you unto myself; that where I am, there ye may be also" (John 14:2–3). As far as I know, that is the first time this truth is revealed in the Bible. And Paul developed it in 1 Thessalonians 4.

However, in the fifth chapter he is speaking of something which was well known in the Old Testament.

"When they shall say, Peace and safety; then sudden destruction cometh upon them." It is going to be a big surprise to the world. They are not going to expect it. I believe that the "big lie," which we will see in the second chapter of 2 Thessalonians, is the promise of peace and safety. The Lord Jesus warned of that: "Take heed that no man deceive you." The world expects to enter a great era of peace, the Millennium, but they will find themselves plunged into the Great Tribulation, which will include the greatest war the world has ever seen. It will come upon them suddenly like a thief in the night.

> **But ye, brethren, are not in darkness, that that day should overtake you as a thief.**
>
> **Ye are all the children of light, and the children of the day: we are not of the night, nor of darkness [1 Thess. 5:4-5].**

The rapture of the church actually does two things: (1) It ends this day of grace in which we are today, this calling out a people for His name and bringing many sons home to glory. This is what God is doing in our day. The Rapture not only ends that, but (2) it begins the Day of the Lord. The Great Tribulation will get under way when the church leaves the earth. The one event of the Rapture will end the day of grace and begin the Day of the Lord. It closes one day and opens another.

"But ye, brethren, are not in darkness, that that day should overtake you as a thief." Why won't it? Well, because we won't be here. We found in chapter 4 that "the Lord himself shall descend from heaven with a shout" and take His church out of the world.

"Ye are all the children of light." In other words, you don't belong to that dispensation which is coming in the future. You belong to the dispensation of grace in which we are today.

Friend, if you do not learn these distinctions which are made in the Scripture, you will be hopelessly confused. I know of no one so hopelessly confused as some theologians in seminaries today. I've talked to them. One man told me that he had simply given up on the study of prophecy and would have nothing to do with it. Why? Because he was not willing to sit down and study the entire Scriptures.

When the Day of the Lord comes, we are going to be with the Lord. We are not in darkness. That day will not overtake us as a thief in the night. He does not come as a thief to take His church. The church is looking for that blessed hope and the glorious appearing of our great God and Savior.

Now Paul gives the admonition to the believers—

> **Therefore let us not sleep, as do others; but let us watch and be sober [1 Thess. 5:6].**

You see, the rapture of the church, that blessed hope, could take place at any time. Because of this, we should not be sleeping Christians.

I heard a song leader down in Georgia, who, in his very quaint way, uttered a great many wise sayings. He was right on target with his remarks. He said, "We are now going to sing 'Standing on the Promises.' There are a lot of folk today who are singing 'Standing on the Promises,' but they are just *sitting on the premises!*" And some of them are actually sleeping pillars in the church today.

Now Paul is saying that, in view of the fact that the Lord Jesus is going to take His church out of the world before that awful period of tribulation, "let us not sleep, as do others; but let us watch and be sober."

The word *sober* has several meanings. It can mean "to stay sober" in the sense of not using an alcoholic stimulant, but there are also other kinds of drunkenness besides that caused by alcohol or drugs. A lot of people get drunk on power or on the making of money or on the pleasures of this world. The child of God is to stay sober and is to watch. Why? Because these tremendous events are to take place in the future.

I believe we are close to the time of the return of the Lord. I don't know, of course, but I think we are. And I know I can say with Paul: ". . . for now is our salvation nearer than when we believed" (Rom. 13:11).

> **For they that sleep sleep in the night; and they that be drunken are drunken in the night.**
>
> **But let us, who are of the day, be sober, putting on the breastplate of faith and love; and for an helmet, the hope of salvation [1 Thess. 5:7-8].**

Again he mentions the word *sober*. Let's understand that we have a duty to perform.

"Putting on the breastplate of faith and love; and for an helmet, the hope of salvation." This speaks of a soldier's duty and is a call to that kind of duty. The breastplate of faith and love is to cover the heart, the vital part of the body. The helmet is the hope of salvation. As I write this, it isn't the style for men or women to wear hats—most people today go bareheaded—but it should be the style for every Christian to wear the helmet of the hope of salvation.

"Faith . . . love . . . hope"—this is now the third time these key words have appeared in this epistle: the labor of love, the work of faith, the patience of hope. Faith is a saving faith, and a saving faith produces works. Calvin said, "Faith alone saves, but the faith that saves is not alone." "Faith" looks to the past when we accepted the Lord Jesus Christ. "Love" is for the present, which is the relationship the believer should have with those around him. The "hope of salvation" is that blessed hope of the future. We are not looking for the Great Tribulation period. I don't see how there could be any rejoicing in that! We are looking for that blessed hope, which is the consummation of our salvation.

John writes, "Beloved, now are we the sons of God, and it doth not yet appear what we shall be: but we know that, when he shall appear, we shall be like him; for we shall see him as he is" (1 John 3:2). God is not through with me, so don't you be impatient with me. A little lady down in West Texas in a testimony meeting said, "Most Christians ought to have written on their backs, 'This is not the best that the grace of God can do.'" I know that I ought to have that written on my back. Since He is not through with me yet, don't be impatient with me, and I won't be impatient with you—because I don't think He is through with you either. Today we have "the hope of salvation," which is that He will consummate that which He has begun in us. "Being confident of this very thing, that he which hath begun a good work in you will perform it until the day of Jesus Christ" (Phil. 1:6).

For God hath not appointed us to wrath, but to obtain salvation by our Lord Jesus Christ [1 Thess. 5:9].

"God hath not appointed us to wrath"—that ought to be clear even to amillennialists, but for some reason they miss the point. God hasn't appointed us to the day of wrath, the Great Tribulation. It is a time of judgment, and the church is not going through it because Christ bore our judgment.

Perhaps you are saying, "McGee, do you think you are good enough to be taken out in the Rapture?" No, I'm not even good enough to be saved. But God saved me by His grace, and when He comes to take His church out of the world, I'm going along with all the super-duper saints—because of the grace of God.

"But to obtain salvation by our Lord Jesus Christ." God has not destined us for wrath, for the Great Tribulation, but for salvation through our Lord Jesus Christ.

> **Who died for us, that, whether we wake or sleep, we should live together with him [1 Thess. 5:10].**

Whether we die first or whether we live until His coming, we shall live together with Him. Most of the church has already gone through the doorway of death. What a parade that will be someday—beginning with Stephen and the apostles, the martyrs, all those who have fallen asleep in Jesus down through the years, and then those who are still alive at His coming, and if you and I are still alive, we will bring up the rear. Thank God, we shall be there by the grace of God!

Now what will these wonderful truths do for you? The next verse tells us: "Wherefore comfort yourselves together." What a comfort all of this is to us as believers!

COMMANDMENTS FOR CHRISTIANS

We come now to a series of twenty-two commandments for Christians. These are the commandments for believers—not just ten of them but twenty-two of them! Up to the time we are saved, God has us shut up to a cross. That is, God is not asking anything of us except this question: "What will you do with My Son who died for you?" After we have accepted Jesus Christ as our Savior, then God talks to us about our lives. The child of God is not under the Ten Commandments as the way of life—he is way above it. He is to live on a much higher plane, as we can see by the commandments in this section. These commandments are practical—right down where the rubber meets the road. It is a wonderful, glorious thing to keep looking for the coming of Christ, but it is also very important that we keep walking down here on the sidewalks of life—at home, in the office, in the schoolroom, wherever we are called to walk.

The Lord Jesus said, "If ye love me, keep my commandments" (John 14:15). There are some Christians who have never listened to His commandments. Well, here are twenty-two of them. They are given like military orders, brief and terse. They are barked out like a second lieutenant would give them to you. We were just told to be sober and to put on the uniform of warfare (see v. 8). Now the orders are given, and they seem to be categorized—that is, certain ones are related to each other.

> **Wherefore comfort yourselves together, and edify one another, even as also ye do [1 Thess. 5:11].**

The first commandment is to "comfort yourselves together," which means to encourage one another in the faith.

The second commandment is to "edify one another." The Thessalonian believers were already doing that, Paul says. *Edify* means "to build up one another." You and I should be a team working together, edifying each other with the Word of God.

> **And we beseech you, brethren, to know them which labour among you, and are over you in the Lord, and admonish you;**
>
> **And to esteem them very highly in love for their work's sake. And be at peace among yourselves [1 Thess. 5:12–13].**

Here are three commandments that seem to belong together. "Know" or understand those who teach the Word of God. It means we should recognize them. When Paul wrote this, he was speaking to the local situation in Thessalonica. He had been with them less than a month. He had won them to Christ and had taught them. A church had been started, we would say, "from scratch." There wasn't a believer there before Paul had arrived and presented the gospel to them (see Acts 17:2–3). So all the Thessalonian believers had come to know Christ at about the same time. Now among them certain ones would have been given the gift of teaching. Some would have the gift of preaching and some of helping. Every believer receives a gift when he is saved, and that gift is to be exercised in the body of believers to build up the body of believers. But I have a notion that among the believers in Thessalonica there could have been this attitude: *So-and-so and I were saved at the same time. I knew him before he was a believer. Where did he get the idea that he could teach me?* So Paul is telling them that certain men and women had been given certain gifts of leadership, and they should respect them. They should look to them for admonition.

We still have the problem today that very few people in the church pay any attention to the teachers God has given them. People say they believe the Bible is the Word of God and they believe every word of it. Then why don't they obey it? Why don't they listen when it is being taught? One man said to me very candidly, "I believe the Bible from cover to cover, and I am ignorant of what is between the covers." Now that is an untenable position to hold. I think if people knew what was between the covers, they *would* believe it. But it is a hypocritical position to say you believe it and then be ignorant of what it says. Anyone who says he believes the Bible is the Word of God is obligated to know what it says. Therefore, those who are preaching and teaching the Word of God should have the attention of the believers.

Now the fourth commandment is "to esteem them very highly in love for their work's sake." I have always appreciated people who love the Word of God because I have found that they become my friends. One of the things I have so appreciated about my radio ministry is the number of friends that God has raised up for me across this country. Many of them have written to say their home is open to me (of course, I can't accept all those invitations), but when I am in their town, they do nice things for me. They reveal their love. When they reveal that love to me—and I'm *hard* to love—it reveals that they honor the Word of God since I teach the Word of God.

Then the fifth commandment: "And be at peace among yourselves." These all come together in one package. You can't have everybody running the church. You can't have everybody running any kind of organization. There must be a certain one with authority.

I think one of the great problems in many churches today is a case of the old bromide, "too many cooks spoil the broth." There needs to be one who is the leader and who is followed. With that arrangement you can have peace. But when everybody is trying to play his own tune, you have anything but harmony and peace!

Now here are the sixth through the ninth commandments—

> **Now we exhort you, brethren, warn them that are unruly, comfort the feebleminded, support the weak, be patient toward all men [1 Thess. 5:14].**

"Warn them that are unruly." This would naturally follow the fifth commandment: "Be at peace among yourselves." The "unruly" are those who are out of step. My feeling is that they are loners, and they like to do their own little thing rather than support the work which God is doing. They are to be warned.

"Comfort the feebleminded." What does he mean by "feebleminded"? Well, a better word would be *fainthearted*. He is not referring to folk with mental problems. But here are folk who are fearful to move out for God, and they need encouraging. There is many a saint today who needs someone to put his arm around him and say, "Brother, you're going to make it. I'm *for* you and I am praying for you." My, what comfort and encouragement that would be to the fearful, the fainthearted—and sometimes all of us get discouraged and become fainthearted!

"Support the weak" is the eighth commandment. There are folk who are weak in the faith. They *cannot* get in step because they are little babies. They are not able to march with the rest; so *help* them. Lift them up, and carry them along.

"Be patient toward all men." That means: Don't lose your temper. That is so difficult! In business or in our other relationships with people, we meet ungodly, unholy, cantankerous, unsaved people who are definitely trying to trip us or to abuse us in some way, and it becomes very difficult to be patient and not to lose our tempers. But God commands us to be patient with everybody.

> **See that none render evil for evil unto any man; but ever follow that which is good, both among yourselves, and to all men [1 Thess. 5:15].**

Now here is the tenth commandment: "See that none render evil for evil unto any man." In other words, don't fight one another.

The eleventh—"but ever follow that which is good, both among yourselves, and to all men." There are three philosophies of life or three standards of conduct. The pagan world operates on a philosophy which does evil in spite of good. In other words, you get the other fellow before he gets you. Use any kind of method. He may have treated you well, but if you can get the advantage over him, do that. That is pagan and heathen philosophy.

Then there is the standard of the so-called refined, cultured, and educated world. That is, do good to those who do good to you. The political parties in our country operate on that principle. If one person helps a man to get into political office, the politician reciprocates by offering the man a job or office. You take care of your own. That is the philosophy of the so-called civilized world. Jesus said, "And if ye do good to them which do good to you, what thank have ye? for sinners also do even the same" (Luke 6:33).

The Christian is to live under a different standard. We are to do good to those who do evil to us. That is contrary to the natural man. The minute someone hits us, we just naturally want to hit him back. This is the philosophy that Paul is talking about—"See that none render evil for evil unto any man; but ever follow that which is good"— even to those who do evil to you.

Now the twelfth commandment—

Rejoice evermore [1 Thess. 5:16].

I think these next three commandments go together. "Rejoice" does not mean to be happy. This is not the happy hour that he is talking about—*happy* is not a New Testament word. This is a *joy* in the Lord as Paul wrote to the Philippians, "Rejoice in the Lord alway: and again I say, Rejoice" (Phil. 4:4). My, what a commandment! You won't find that in the Ten Commandments! The child of God has no right to go around with a sour puss. The child of God has no right to be a cantankerous individual. If you a child of God, you are to *rejoice* evermore! That, incidentally, is a fruit of the Holy Spirit—love, *joy*, peace. If you cannot rejoice, then begin reading the Word of God and calling on God to put joy in your heart. He will do it.

Pray without ceasing [1 Thess. 5:17].

This has to do with an attitude of prayer. I don't think this means that one is to stay on his knees all the time. But it means to pray regularly and to be constantly in the attitude of prayer.

Associated with that is this fourteenth commandment—

In every thing give thanks: for this is the will of God in Christ Jesus concerning you [1 Thess. 5:18].

This tells us to "give thanks" in all circumstances, not just once a year, but all the time.

This "is the will of God in Christ Jesus concerning you." If you come to me and ask what is the will of God for you, I can tell you three specific things that are the will of God for you: Rejoice always, pray without ceasing, and give thanks in everything. That is the will of God for you.

Now the fifteenth—

Quench not the Spirit [1 Thess. 5:19].

One of the figures that is used for the Holy Spirit is fire. How do you quench a fire? You dampen it down and don't let it burn. To quench the Spirit means that you refuse to do the will of God; that is, you are not listening to the Holy Spirit. You refuse to let the Holy Spirit be your Guide to lead you. You and I quench the Holy Spirit when we take matters into our own hands.

This is the same teaching that Paul gave to the Ephesian believers: "And grieve not the holy Spirit of God, whereby ye are sealed unto the day of redemption" (Eph. 4:30). You cannot grieve a *thing*; you grieve a *Person*. The Holy Spirit is a Person, and He is grieved by sin in our lives. Also, He is quenched when we step out of the will of God.

Despise not prophesyings [1 Thess. 5:20].

Do not look down upon Bible study as something that is beneath you. Do not be indifferent to the Word of God. We have a lot of folk who are in Christian service, but they are ignorant of the Bible and they look down on Bible study. Occasionally I hear such a person saying, "You just spend all your time in Bible study and you don't do anything. What you need to do is get out and get busy." Well, what is needed is to get busy studying the Word of God, and after you do that you will see how to get busy and really be *effective*.

We had a Bible study downtown in Los Angeles, averaging fifteen hundred people every Thursday night over a period of twenty-one years—what a thrill that was! What a privilege that was! But sometimes folk would make a remark like, "You need to get out and do something, not just go to sit and listen to the Bible." The interesting thing is that those people who came to sit and listen to the Bible *did* go out and do something. There are several hundred of those people who are out on the mission field; there are several hundred who are witnessing for God; and there are several hundred in the ministry. I notice that the boys who do not study the Word of God run down like an eight-day clock. Their ministries don't last too long. The sixteenth commandment which Paul gives the Thessalonians is "despise not prophesyings," that is, the teaching of the Word of God.

Prove all things; hold fast that which is good [1 Thess. 5:21].

"Prove all things." Don't be taken in. To put it crudely, don't be a sucker. Don't be misled into supporting a project just because somebody sends you a picture of pathetic looking orphans. Don't contribute to things you know nothing about. Don't fall for some promotion job. Investigate. Investigate anything to which you give your support. Christians ought not to be gullible. We are to prove all things. This also means that we are not to be taken in by flattery. There are many deceivers in the world.

"Hold fast that which is good." Hold to that which is true and genuine.

Abstain from all appearance of evil [1 Thess. 5:22].

This nineteenth commandment is the answer for questionable pastimes and amusements. If there is any question in your mind whether something is right or wrong, then it is wrong for you. Abstain from all *appearance* of evil.

Now notice that man is a truine being—

> **And the very God of peace sanctify you wholly; and I pray God your whole spirit and soul and body be preserved blameless unto the coming of our Lord Jesus Christ [1 Thess. 5:23].**

Man is a triune being; body, soul (mind), and spirit. "Sanctify you wholly"—not perfectly, but we are to reach a place of maturation. We should not continue to be babes in Christ; we should be growing to maturity.

> **Faithful is he that calleth you, who also will do it [1 Thess. 5:24].**

You can depend upon God.

> **Brethren, pray for us [1 Thess. 5:25].**

This twentieth command is to pray for those who give out the gospel. You can't pray for Paul today, but you can pray for me, and I would appreciate it. You can pray for your pastor and your missionaries. I know they would appreciate it also.

Greet all the brethren with an holy kiss [1 Thess. 5:26].

This is a commandment, too. Just make sure it is a *holy* kiss! In our culture and with our customs, a warm handshake will do.

I charge you by the Lord that this epistle be read unto all the holy brethren [1 Thess. 5:27].

That is the twenty-second commandment, and I have obeyed it by quoting this entire epistle to you!

The grace of our Lord Jesus Christ be with you. Amen [1 Thess. 5:28].

And I pray that the grace of our Lord Jesus Christ may be with you my beloved.

(For Bibliography to 1 Thessalonians, see Bibliography at the end of 2 Thessalonians.)

2 THESSALONIANS

The Second Epistle to the
THESSALONIANS

INTRODUCTION

The second epistle followed shortly after the first epistle in A.D. 52 or 53.

The Christians in Thessalonica were still baby Christians when Paul wrote 2 Thessalonians. His first letter to them had given rise to further questions, and Paul is attempting to answer them in his second letter. There was circulating in the Thessalonian church a letter or report, purported to have come from Paul, which was inclined to disturb the Christians. This false report claimed that Christ had already come and had already gathered out the church to Himself, and that the world was then living in the judgments of the "day of the Lord." These people were being persecuted, as we saw in the first epistle. They were suffering for the gospel's sake, and it was easy for them to believe that they had entered the Great Tribulation period, and that all of the believers (not only the dead) had missed the Rapture. Paul attempts to allay their fears by writing this epistle and stating definitely that "our gathering together unto him" is yet future (2 Thess. 2:1), and that "the day of the Lord" has certain forerunners which must first come: the apostasy and the "man of sin" must come first. Therefore they could reasonably believe they were not in the Great Tribulation.

Paul says that the outward organization of the professing church is going to go into total apostasy. In Luke 18:8 the Lord asked, ". . . when the Son of man cometh, shall he find faith on the earth?" The way the question is couched in the Greek it demands a negative answer. He will not find the faith on the earth when He comes again. The organized church will be in total apostasy. This is confirmed in the Book of Revelation. In the fourth chapter the church has been removed from the earth, and nothing is left but an empty shell of an organization that has a form of godliness but denies the power of it. That same organization is the great harlot in chapter 17 of Revelation, which is about as frightful a picture as you will find in the Word of God.

The Thessalonian believers thought they had entered the Great Tribulation period, and ever since that time folk who have gone through persecutions and tribulations have believed that they were in the Great Tribulation period. For example, during World War II at the time of the blitz in Britain, some of the British ministers who were conservative in their faith came to the conclusion that they had entered the Great Tribulation and that the church was going to go through it.

A good friend of mine, a preacher from England, believes that the church will go through the Tribulation. In fact, he believes the church is in it right now. Well, he is living in California now, and one day we were having lunch together with a mutual friend who was a layman, who had bought us big T-bone steaks. The subject of the church and the Tribulation came up, and he insisted that the church was in the Great Tribulation. To confirm his argument he said, "McGee, if you had been in Great Britain during the blitz, and night after night had gone down into the subways with your people, the members of your church, and practically every night one person would have a nervous breakdown because of the strain, and would have to be taken the next day to the country, you would share my belief." I said to him, "If I had been in Great Britain, and in the blitz as you were, I am convinced that I would have thought as you did, *Boy, this is the Great Tribulation!* But after the war was over if I had come to the United States and was having lunch with a couple of friends and was eating a T-bone steak, I think I would pinch myself and ask myself, *Is this really the Great Tribulation period?* If this is the Tribulation, let's have more of it since it will mean more T-bone steaks." He looked at me and said in that British disdainful voice, "McGee, you are being ridiculous!" So I told him that I didn't think I was being ridiculous; I thought *he* was being ridiculous.

The description of the Tribulation in the Bible is much worse than anything that happened during World War II. This period has been so clearly identified by Christ that there is no reason for getting panicky and for being stampeded into an unwarranted position. Christ said that there is coming a small interval which will be blocked off by ". . . such as was not since the beginning of the world to this time, no, nor ever shall be" (Matt. 24:21). Nothing like it has taken place before, and nothing like it will ever take place afterward.

While 1 Thessalonians emphasized the return of Christ for His church in what we call the "Rapture," 2 Thessalonians emphasizes the return of Christ to the earth the second time, when He returns in judgment and sets up His Kingdom here upon this earth. This is called the *revelation*. You see, at the Rapture, the emphasis is not upon His coming to earth, because He doesn't come to the *earth*. He makes it clear that "we shall be caught up to meet the Lord in the *air*" (see 1 Thess. 4:17). "Caught up" is the Greek word *harpazō*, meaning "to snatch away." We shall be snatched away or raptured to meet Christ in the air. However, the revelation of Christ is when He returns to the earth to set up His Kingdom. In the time gap between these two events will be the Great Tribulation period.

As we saw in 1 Thessalonians, the Rapture is not a subject of the Old Testament; that teaching does not appear in the Old Testament. The hope of the Old Testament saints was an earthly hope. They were looking for their Messiah to come and establish a kingdom here upon this earth—which would be heaven upon earth. The expression "Kingdom of Heaven" means the reign of the heavens over the earth. That is putting it as simply as I know how. Some of the theologians really have made it complicated—so complicated that I wonder if they are trying to establish some kind of a theory. But the Kingdom of Heaven which Jesus talked about is the reign of the heavens over the earth, because this earth is going to become a heaven when He is here.

OUTLINE

CHAPTER 1

THEME: Persecution of believers now and judgment of unbelievers hereafter (at Christ's coming)

INTRODUCTION

Paul, and Silvanus, and Timotheus, unto the church of the Thessalonians in God our Father and the Lord Jesus Christ [2 Thess. 1:1].

Paul's greeting is his usual friendly greeting to a church which is theologically and spiritually sound. Paul includes the greetings of Silas (a contraction of the name Silvanus) and Timothy (Timotheus is the Greek form). These three men had endured a great deal for the sake of the gospel. Paul and Silas were in the prison at Philippi. Paul, Silas, and Timothy had gone to Thessalonica together, and later Paul had to leave them. He waited for them in Athens and, when they did not come, he went on to Corinth where they finally met. It was at that time Paul wrote his first epistle to the Thessalonians to answer some of the questions that had come up since he had been there.

When Paul writes his second epistle, he identifies his two co-workers who are brethren with him. He would identify himself with men who, for us today, would be totally unknown had not Paul included them in these epistles. This reveals something of the character of Paul. A man who had been a proud young Pharisee has become a humble follower of the Lord Jesus Christ and a servant of His and an apostle of His.

"Unto the church of the Thessalonians." That was the local church in Thessalonica. Paul believed in the local church, and that church in Thessalonica was "in God our Father and the Lord Jesus Christ." He probably did not mention the Holy Spirit because the Spirit was in the church in Thessalonica indwelling the believers. The indwelling Spirit enabled them to manifest the life of Christ and to walk worthy of the high calling of God. Their position, however, was in God the

Father and in the Lord Jesus Christ. This means, my friend, that Paul taught the deity of Christ. There was no doubt in Paul's mind that Jesus Christ was God the Son.

In John 10:27–29 the Lord Jesus said, "My sheep hear my voice, and I know them, and they follow me: And I give unto them eternal life; and they shall never perish, neither shall any man pluck them out of my hand. My Father, which gave them me, is greater than all; and no man is able to pluck them out of my Father's hand." In this first verse you have the two hands of deity which belong to the Lord Jesus and God the Father. That is where the church is positionally—the Thessalonian church was there, and I hope your church is there. The important thing is not the name of your church. The important thing is that you and other true believers are in Christ Jesus, and that makes the local church very important. The Holy Spirit indwells true believers, and by His power they can manifest Christ in the local neighborhood, in the community, in the town, in the state, and in the world, showing forth the life of God. That is what Paul is saying to these believers in his introduction.

> **Grace unto you, and peace, from God our Father and the Lord Jesus Christ [2 Thess. 1:2].**

Grace and peace are two important words in the gospel. Grace comes first. If you have experienced the grace of God, that means you have been saved. "For by grace are ye saved through faith; and that not of yourselves: it is the gift of God: Not of works, lest any man should boast" (Eph. 2:8–9). When you come to God as a lost sinner, bringing nothing, and receiving everything from Him, then you have experienced the grace of God. He offers you salvation—the gift of God is eternal life. You cannot work for a gift, and if you do, it ceases to be a gift and it becomes something you have earned. It becomes a payment. God is not patting you on the back because you are a nice Sunday school boy. Salvation is God offering you, a lost, hell-doomed sinner, eternal life if you trust Christ. That is grace.

"Peace"—if you have experienced God's grace, then you know something about His peace. Peace is the world's softest pillow that you can sleep on at night. It is the peace that comes when you know that your sins are forgiven. Peace comes, not from some psychological gyrations you go through, or through the counsel of a psychiatrist, but it comes from a supernatural source—from "God our Father and the Lord Jesus Christ"; it is supernatural. If you don't have it, you *can* have it, because it is the gift of God which is given to sinners who turn to Christ.

PERSECUTION OF BELIEVERS AND FRUITS OF IT

We are bound to thank God always for you, brethren, as it is meet, because that your faith groweth exceedingly, and the charity of every one of you all toward each other aboundeth [2 Thess. 1:3].

The word *charity* in this verse is "love." In verse 4 Paul speaks of patience and faith. In verses 3 and 4 we have that little trinity that Paul uses: faith, love, and patience. These three words are abstract terms, but we must bring them out of the abstract into the concrete. Get them walking on the sidewalks today. This again is the "work of faith" which Paul mentioned in 1 Thessalonians 1:3. Saving faith produces works. A saving faith will produce a love in the heart for God's children. My friend, if you are a child of God, you will have to love me whether or not you want to, and I'm going to have to love you. It is a wonderful arrangement!

In the next verse Paul picks up the third word, which he uses with "love" and "faith." It is "patience." This is not the patience of waiting in a traffic jam or waiting for a light to turn green. It is the patience that is willing to live for God and accept whatever He sends your way, knowing that all things do work together for good. It is the patience that has as its goal coming into God's presence someday. This enables you to get over the rough places that come into your life. The life of a Christian reminds me of traveling over a highway. Many years ago I used to cross the country by automobile from Texas to California. There would be many places where a detour sign would put us on a rough old road. But along the way we would see a sign that read "5 miles to the double highway," and the rough road became a little bit smoother by knowing that we would hit the asphalt or the concrete in a little while. And many of us are on a detour in this life. The road is rough, and we are called upon to suffer. Well, if you have a good view of the future, it will give you the patience of hope—a hope that looks way down yonder to the good smooth road coming up. And it may be closer than you think.

"We are bound to thank God always for you, brethren, as it is meet." The word *meet* means "proper"—it is right and fitting for us to thank God for you.

"Because that your faith groweth exceedingly, and the charity [love] of every one of you all toward each other aboundeth." You cannot grow toward God without growing outward toward your brother. When you grow toward God in grace and knowledge and faith, you grow toward your brother in love.

And God must send us a little trouble because that is the discipline which produces patience in our lives. It enables us to look down into the future with hope.

So that we ourselves glory in you in the churches of God for your patience and faith in all your persecutions and tribulations that ye endure [2 Thess. 1:4].

"Tribulations" are afflictions. The church will not go through the Great Tribulation, but we will go through the little tribulation. We all will have trouble down here. If you are not having any troubles, then there must be something wrong with you, because the Lord disciplines His children.

Patience is an interesting word. The Greek word translated by the English word *patience* has the literal meaning of "standing under." It means to be placed under. A great many people try to get out from *under* the problems and difficulties. The person who is patient is able to stay under, and he keeps on carrying the load. He doesn't throw it off; he doesn't try to get rid of his responsibility.

These Thessalonian Christians had a real testimony in the Roman world of that day. (Thessalonica was a Roman colony, and people were going to and fro from that colony, so the word got out everywhere.) The patience and faith of these Christians were unshaken as they were enduring a great deal of trouble, persecutions, and afflictions.

Trouble is not something strange. The Word of God makes it clear that we are going to have trouble in this life. Peter expressed it like this: "Beloved, think it not strange concerning the fiery trial which is to try you, as though some strange thing happened unto you" (1 Pet. 4:12). Sometimes we hear Christians say, "I don't know why God let this happen to me. Nobody else has ever had to go through this." It is safe to say that such a statement is not true. Whatever you are going through, you have company. It is not a strange thing for suffering to come to us. Peter goes on to say, "But rejoice, inasmuch as ye are partakers of Christ's sufferings; that, when his glory shall be revealed, ye may be glad also with exceeding joy" (1 Pet. 4:13). Peter warns that Christians sometimes get themselves into trouble. "But let none of you suffer as a murderer, or as a thief, or as an evildoer, or as a busybody in other men's matters" (1 Pet. 4:15). A Christian can get himself in hot water because he talks too much—talking about others. Or he can suffer persecution because he is dishonest. There is no advantage to that kind of suffering. That is not the discipline in life which will develop patience. That is simply getting what you have coming to you. Peter goes on, "Yet if any man suffer as a Christian, let him not be ashamed; but let him glorify God on this behalf" (1 Pet. 4:16). There is a difference between being disciplined to learn patience and the punishment of the wicked. God disciplines His children for their development, for their growth, that they might have patience and a hope for the future. We don't need to get too comfortable down here. When we do, we no longer have the hope before us of the Lord's return.

> **Which is a manifest token of the righteous judgment of God, that ye may be counted worthy of the kingdom of God, for which ye also suffer [2 Thess. 1:5].**

Our suffering has nothing to do with salvation, but it sure prepares us for our eternal state. When you and I look back to this life on earth, maybe some of us will wish that we had had a little bit more discipline than we got!

While the judgment of the wicked begins with verse 8, this is certainly the introduction to it.

> **Seeing it is a righteous thing with God to recompense tribulation to them that trouble you [2 Thess. 1:6].**

When God judges, God is righteous in it. Paul asks the question: "Is there unrighteousness with God?" The answer is, Let it not be—"God forbid" (see Rom. 9:14). Whatever God does is absolutely right. He can do no wrong. Sometimes we complain about the things that happen to us because we are ignorant; we do not understand God's ways. But God has a very definite purpose for all that He does. And God is righteous in sending the Great Tribulation. It is a judgment of sinners.

> **And to you who are troubled rest with us, when the Lord Jesus shall be revealed from heaven with his mighty angels [2 Thess. 1:7].**

The Lord Jesus is coming in judgment.

JUDGMENT OF WICKED AT CHRIST'S COMING

> **In flaming fire taking vengeance on them that know not God, and that obey not the gospel of our Lord Jesus Christ:**

> **Who shall be punished with everlasting destruction from the presence of the Lord, and from the glory of his power [2 Thess. 1:8–9].**

The Word of God actually says very little about heaven. One of the reasons is that it is so wonderful we could not comprehend it. And the Lord does not want us to get so heavenly minded that we are no earthly good. He wants us to keep our eyes on our pathway down here, and I think He wants us to keep our noses to the grindstone much of the time. In other words, He has a purpose for our lives on earth, and He wants us to fulfill that purpose.

Scripture not only says very little about heaven, it says *less* about the condition of the lost. It is so awful that the Holy Spirit has drawn a veil over it. There is nothing given to satisfy the morbid curiosity or the lust for revenge. When God judges, He does not do it in a vindictive manner. He does it in order to vindicate His righteousness and His holiness. There is nothing in the Scriptures to satisfy our curiosity about hell, but there is enough said to give us a warning. It does not mean that it is less real because so little is said. Actually, Christ Himself said more about hell than did anyone else. Hell is an awful reality. I am not going to speculate about it; I'm just quoting what is said right here: He is coming "in flaming fire taking vengeance on them that know not God, and that obey not the gospel of our Lord Jesus Christ: who shall be punished with everlasting destruction from the presence of the Lord, and from the glory of his power."

Hell is ridiculed today, but that does not mean it doesn't exist. Our beliefs are sometimes only wishful thinking. For example, it was the popular notion that Hitler would not plunge Europe into a war and turn Europe into a holocaust of flaming fire. But he did. Chamberlain, the man with the umbrella, went over to meet with Hitler and Mussolini, and he came back saying that we would have peace in our time. Well, we didn't have peace, and we don't have peace in the world today. Also, many people thought that Japan would never attack America. Our government did not believe she would, and the liberal churches at that time were teaching pacifism. Well, whether they believed it or not, there was a vicious attack at Pearl Harbor.

Friend, we might as well face the fact that there is a hell. Christ is returning to this earth some day. First He will take His own out of the earth, and then His coming will be a terror to the wicked; it will be a judgment upon those who "know not God, and that obey not the gospel of our Lord Jesus Christ." "And this is life eternal, that they might know thee the only true God, and Jesus Christ, whom thou hast sent"

(John 17:3). Do you want to work for your salvation? Jesus said, ". . . This is the work of God, that ye believe on him whom he hath sent" (John 6:29). That is what the Word of God teaches.

I know that it is not popular to talk about hell and judgment. Even the Christian testimonies that we hear and read are filled with I, I, I— "I became successful in business. I saved my marriage. My personality changed." Nothing very much is said about the Lord Jesus. How many testimonies have you heard in which it is said, "I was a hell-doomed sinner going straight to hell, I was lost, and He saved me"? The important thing to say in a testimony is not what He has given you but from what He has delivered you. That was the whole purpose for the coming of our Savior. He came to redeem us! He didn't come to give us new personalities or to make us successful. He came to *deliver* us from *hell!* That's not popular to say. Folk don't like to hear it.

There are too few people today who are willing to confront folk with the fact that they are lost. Suppose you were asleep in a burning building, and a man rushed into that building to rescue you. He awakened you, picked you up, and carried you bodily out of that burning building. He liked you; so he made you his son. He brought you into his lovely home and gave you many wonderful gifts. Now if you had the opportunity to stand before a group of people and tell about this man and express your appreciation in his presence, what would you thank him for? Would you thank him for making you his son? I hope you would. But wouldn't you really thank him most for the fact that he risked his life to save you out of a burning building? Nothing else would have mattered if he had not rescued you from a flaming death.

Now, my friend, the judgment of the lost is coming. If you want to stay in that class, you shall be judged. Somebody needs to tell you the facts, and I am telling them to you right now.

Again, who are the lost? They are those who (1) "know not God" and who (2) "obey not the gospel of our Lord Jesus Christ." Let me repeat verse 9: "Who shall be punished with everlasting destruction from the presence of the Lord, and from the glory of his power."

When he shall come to be glorified in his saints, and to be admired in all them that believe (because our testi-

mony among you was believed) in that day [2 Thess. 1:10].

The coming of Christ to the earth in judgment will justify the believers who have put their trust in Him, and it will glorify the Savior.

Wherefore also we pray always for you, that our God would count you worthy of this calling, and fulfil all the good pleasure of his goodness, and the work of faith with power:

That the name of our Lord Jesus Christ may be glorified in you, and ye in him, according to the grace of our God and the Lord Jesus Christ [2 Thess. 1:11-12].

"That the name of our Lord Jesus Christ may be glorified in you." If God has prospered you, made you a financial success, and you can glorify Christ, that's fine. But somehow I am more impressed by a little woman who has been flat on her back in a hospital most of her life—yet has a radiant testimony for Christ. Certainly Christ is being glorified in her.

CHAPTER 2

THEME: The program for the world in connection with Christ's coming

Back in 1 Thessalonians, beginning at verse 13 of chapter 4, we called attention to the rapture of the church; we also spoke of the Day of the Lord, the Great Tribulation, and the coming of Christ in glory to this earth. In this epistle the emphasis is going to be on the Great Tribulation period, but we are also going to find one of the finest passages on the rapture of the church.

THE RAPTURE OCCURS FIRST

Now we beseech you, brethren, by the coming of our Lord Jesus Christ, and by our gathering together unto him [2 Thess. 2:1].

"Our gathering together unto him" is the rapture of the church. The first aspect of Christ's coming is in view in this verse. There is no judgment at this time.

THE DAY OF THE LORD FOLLOWS THE RAPTURE

That ye be not soon shaken in mind, or be troubled, neither by spirit, nor by word, nor by letter as from us, as that the day of Christ is at hand [2 Thess. 2:2].

In many good Bibles with notes you will find the note in the margin—if it has not already been changed in the text—that this should read "the day of the Lord is at hand" rather than "the day of Christ is at hand." The Day of the Lord has no reference to the church. After the Rapture, the day of Christ, or the age of grace, comes to an end and the Day of the Lord begins. The Day of the Lord is a subject which is often mentioned in the Old Testament, whereas the Rapture is not. The Day of the Lord begins with night. Joel tells us it is darkness and not light. It is a time of judgment. It opens with night just like every Hebrew day opens: "the evening and the morning were the first day" (Gen. 1:5, italics mine).

"Nor by word, nor by letter"—apparently someone had been circulating a letter or an oral word among the Thessalonians that the Day of the Lord had come. It is interesting that there is always a group of super-duper saints who seem to think they get direct information from the Lord. They don't think they need to study the Word of God; they imagine they get their information directly through dreams or visions or special revelations. Now, friend, I admit that it is much easier to pick up all your information in a telephone conversation than it is to go to school or take up the Bible and study it, but it won't be coming straight from God. So there was circulating in Thessalonica a word that had come to them, and it was a special "revelation," something that Brother Paul had not told them.

"Nor by letter" would indicate that a spurious letter had been circulating. Or perhaps someone simply said they had seen such a letter.

"Nor by letter as from us" would mean that they said the letter supposedly came from Paul, Timothy, and Silas.

The word they circulated was that "the day of the Lord is at hand." This had caused a problem with the Thessalonian believers, and we can see why. They were enduring persecution. Because they were having trouble, it was very easy for someone to say, "Well, this is the Great Tribulation that we are in. The Day of the Lord has come, and we are already in it."

The Day of the Lord is a technical phrase that speaks of the period beginning with the Great Tribulation and continuing through the Millennium. It is a day that begins with judgment. Joel describes the Day of the Lord in some detail in chapter 2 of his prophecy, and Peter quoted him on the Day of Pentecost. His listeners knew that there was a day coming when the Spirit of God would be poured out—but it was the coming Day of the Lord of which they knew. In Acts 2:20 Peter says, "The sun shall be turned into darkness, and the moon into blood, before that great and notable day of the Lord come." Certainly that had not happened at Pentecost. At the crucifixion of Christ there had been an earthquake and darkness, but on the Day of Pentecost there was nothing like that at all. There was a rushing sound like a mighty wind, and it had the appearance of tongues of fire as it rested upon each of those present. There was no wind, but it sounded like a hurricane when it hit the town, and it caused everybody to rush up to the temple area to see what had happened. Peter is saying that the Day of Pentecost was *similar* to the day Joel described: "You think these men are drunk? They are not; they are filled with the Holy Spirit." Because of Joel's prophecy, the orthodox Jews in that day believed there was a day coming when God would pour out His Spirit on *all* flesh—but on the Day of Pentecost it was not poured out on all flesh. The Day of the Lord is yet future.

Peter refers to the Day of the Lord again in his epistle: "But the day of the Lord will come as a thief in the night." We have already seen that for the church He will *not* come as a thief in the night (1 Thess. 5). The church is to be awake and waiting for Him. It is to the sleepy world that He will come as a thief in the night. Peter goes on to say, ". . . in the which the heavens shall pass away with a great noise, and the elements shall melt with fervent heat, the earth also and the works that are therein shall be burned up" (2 Pet. 3:10). Again, this did not happen on the Day of Pentecost.

Another Scripture which shows that the Day of the Lord has no reference to the church is Revelation 6:17: "For the great day of his wrath is come; and who shall be able to stand?" That is not for the church. The church is to look for *Him*—a Person—to come, because we are identified with Him.

> **Let no man deceive you by any means: for that day shall not come, except there come a falling away first, and that man of sin be revealed, the son of perdition [2 Thess. 2:3].**

"Let no man deceive you by any means." If we are not to be deceived, then let's listen to Paul.

"For that day shall not come." Which day? The Day of the Lord—

not the Rapture. The Day of the Lord shall not come except there be the fulfilling of two conditions: (1) "There come a falling away first" and (2) "that man of sin be revealed, the son of perdition." Both of these things must take place before the Day of the Lord can begin, and neither one of them has taken place as yet.

There must be "a falling away first." Many have interpreted this to mean the apostasy, and I agree that it does refer to that. But I think it means more than that, as a careful examination of the word will reveal. The Greek word that is here translated as "falling away" is *apostasia*. The root word actually means "departure or removal from."

Paul says that before the Day of the Lord begins there must first come a removing. There are two kinds of removing that are going to take place. First, the organized church will depart from the faith— that is what we call apostasy. But there will be *total* apostasy when the Lord comes, and that cannot take place until the true church is removed. The Lord asked, ". . . when the Son of man cometh [to the earth], shall he find [the] faith . . . ?" (Luke 18:8). When He says "the faith," He means that body of truth which He left here. The answer to His question is no, He will not find the faith here when He returns. There will be total apostasy because of two things: (1) the organization of the church has departed from the faith—it has apostatized and (2) there has been another departure, the departure of the true church from the earth. The departure of the true church leads into the total apostatizing of the organized church. The Day of the Lord cannot begin—nor the Great Tribulation period—until the departure of the true church has taken place.

Paul is not going into detail about the rapture of the church because he has already written about that in his first epistle: "For the Lord himself shall descend from heaven with a shout, with the voice of the archangel, and with the trump of God: and the dead in Christ shall rise first: Then we which are alive and remain shall be caught up together with them in the clouds, to meet the Lord in the air: and so shall we ever be with the Lord" (1 Thess. 4:16–17). That is the departure, the removal, of the church.

The organized church which is left down here will totally depart from the faith. We see it pictured as the great harlot in Revelation 17.

The Laodicean church, which is the seventh and last church described in the Book of Revelation, is in sad condition. I think that is the period we are in right now. When the true believers are gone, it will get even worse. It will finally end in total apostasy.

From the viewpoint of the earth the removal of believers is a departure. From the viewpoint of heaven, it is a rapture, a snatching or catching up. I think the world is going to say at that time, "Oh, boy, they are gone!" They think that fellow McGee and other Bible teachers are a nuisance, and they will be glad when they are gone. The world will rejoice. They do not realize that it will be a sad day for them. They think they will be entering into the blessing of the Millennium, not realizing they are actually entering into the Great Tribulation period, which will be a time of toruble such as the world has never before seen.

Sometime ago Mrs. McGee and I were at the Los Angeles airport to take a morning flight to Florida. We always go early to have breakfast at the airport. While we were waiting, a big 747 was getting ready to go to the Hawaiian Islands. There was a fine-looking Marine Corps fellow there with his pretty wife and a precious little baby. But they looked so sad. A few minutes later when it came time to board the plane, they stood up. The father put his arms around them both, and they just wept. Then he picked up his bag and disappeared through the gate. It was a departure. It was an *apostasia*, a removal. The young wife picked up the baby and slowly walked back to the escalator, tears running down her face. My heart went out to her. Life would be hard for her now.

I couldn't help but think that that is the way it will be for the world. When the church departs, many people will be glad to see us go. The liberals will be glad to get rid of us. There will be rejoicing. But they do not realize how hard it will be for them. They are going to enter the Great Tribulation period.

The second thing which must happen is that the "man of sin be revealed, the son of perdition." When he is revealed the Great Tribulation period has already begun. Here he is called "the man of sin." John calls him "the antichrist." John is the only one who uses that term, by the way. The Antichrist has about thirty different titles in the Bible.

He is a subject of the Old Testament. He is going to be Satan's man. This is the man who will put the Roman Empire back together again, and he will finally become a world dictator. He is going to deceive the world. He could be in our midst today, but he won't be able to appear in power or reveal who he is until after the Great Tribulation period begins.

Paul tells us more about him—

> **Who opposeth and exalteth himself above all that is called God, or that is worshipped; so that he as God sitteth in the temple of God, shewing himself that he is God [2 Thess. 2:4].**

One of his claims will be that he is God. In Revelation 13 we find that the beast out of the sea (the Antichrist) brings together western Europe, and he will put it back together again. When he does this, he will show himself as God. The world will think that he is Christ. That is the big lie.

> **Remember ye not, that, when I was yet with you, I told you these things? [2 Thess. 2:5].**

Paul hadn't hesitated to talk about these things. Some say that a preacher shouldn't dwell on these topics. Well, Paul did. Paul says, "When I was with you, I told you about him."

MYSTERY OF LAWLESSNESS WORKING TODAY, RESTRAINED BY THE HOLY SPIRIT

> **And now ye know what withholdeth that he might be revealed in his time [2 Thess. 2:6].**

What *can* withhold evil in the world? The only One I know who can do that is the Holy Spirit. Governments can't do it—they are not doing it. The Roman Empire couldn't do it; it was an evil force itself.

> For the mystery of iniquity doth already work: only he
> who now letteth will let, until he be taken out of the way
> [2 Thess. 2:7].

Let me give you a clearer translation of this verse: "For the mystery of lawlessness doth already work: only he who now hinders will hinder, until he be taken out of the way."

"The mystery of lawlessness" had begun to work already in Paul's day, and it continues to work. The Lord Jesus gave a parable in Matthew 13 which reveals the condition of the world today. These are the mysteries of the Kingdom of Heaven, and they explain the condition of the world and of the church in the world today. The Word of God is being sown out in the field of the world, but an enemy has come in and has sown tares. The tares and the wheat are growing together—the Word of God and lawlessness grow together today. The world is getting worse and, in a sense, the world is getting better, because I think the Word of God is going out more than it ever has in the history of the world. The doors are open—the Word is growing, the wheat is growing. But the tares are growing also.

Lawlessness will continue to get worse and worse, but the Holy Spirit will not let Satan go all the way in this age. When the Holy Spirit will be removed, it will be like taking the stopper out of the bottle—the liquid of lawlessness will pour out all over the world in that day.

When will the Holy Spirit be taken out? He will be taken out with the church. Won't the Holy Spirit be in the world during the Great Tribulation? Yes. Wasn't He in the world before Pentecost? He surely was. He was present in the days of the Old Testament, but He was on a different mission. And He will be on a different mission after the church is removed. Now the Spirit of God is sealing us until the day of redemption when He will present us and deliver us to the Lord Jesus. If He didn't do that, we would never make it. After He does that, I believe He will come back to the earth to resume His former mission down here. But He will not hinder evil—He will let the Devil have his day for a while. Believe me, I don't want to be on the earth when the

Devil has it! It looks bad enough to me as it is today; so I don't want to be here when it is turned over to him.

And then shall that Wicked be revealed, whom the Lord shall consume with the spirit of his mouth, and shall destroy with the brightness of his coming [2 Thess. 2:8].

"That Wicked"—the Antichrist, the Man of Sin—will be a world dictator. Nobody can stop him. No power on earth—only the coming of Christ will stop him. As God's people in Egypt were helpless and hopeless until God delivered them, so the believers during the Tribulation will be helpless under the power of the Antichrist until the Lord Jesus comes to the earth to establish His Kingdom. "The Lord shall consume with the spirit of his mouth," that is, the Word of God which is the two-edged sword that proceeds from His mouth shall consume the Antichrist. It was the Word of God that created this universe. All God had to do was to speak. God said, "Let there be light: and there was light" (Gen. 1:3). The Lord Jesus Christ is the living Word of God. Today we have the Bible, which is the written Word of God. The written Word is about the living Word, and it is alive and potent. When the Lord Jesus returns, He comes as the living Word of God.

"And shall destroy with the brightness of his coming." "Brightness" is the Greek word *epiphaneia* or "epiphany" in English, and it refers to the shining forth of His coming. When the Lord Jesus came to Bethlehem, it was His first epiphany. Titus 2:11 uses that word *epiphaneia* when it says, "For the grace of God that bringeth salvation hath *appeared* to all men" (italics mine). That was the gracious appearing of His coming.

As George Macdonald put it:

> "Thou cam'st, a little baby thing,
> That made a woman cry."

When He comes again it will be another epiphany. He will take His church out of the world, and then He is coming to the earth to establish His Kingdom. His first coming had two episodes of coming, if you want to look at it that way. He came to Bethlehem as a little baby, and then later He began His ministry at the age of thirty years when He walked into the temple and cleansed it. His second coming also has two phases. He calls for His church to meet Him in the air, and then He comes down to the earth to establish His Kingdom. At that time the Antichrist shall be consumed and destroyed with the brightness of His coming.

LAWLESS ONE TO APPEAR IN GREAT TRIBULATION

Even him, whose coming is after the working of Satan with all power and signs and lying wonders [2 Thess. 2:9].

This is the Antichrist, Satan's man, the Man of Sin, the lawless one. He will come "after the working of Satan with all power and signs and lying wonders."

"Power" here is *dunamis* in the Greek. It means a physical power whose source is supernatural. He will be quite a healer and a miracle worker. I think he will be able to walk on water. I think he might be able to control the wind. Remember that Satan at one time let a wind destroy the sons and daughters of Job. I am always afraid when anyone tells me of someone who is performing miracles today, because the next miracle worker predicted by the Bible is the one whose coming is after the working of Satan. I am always afraid that miracle workers have not come from heaven. The Devil will send this man with power and signs and lying wonders. That is the reason it is so important for us to get our eyes off men and to get them on Christ, to walk by faith in Him.

"Signs" means tokens. They have the purpose of appealing to the understanding. This man will have signs which will appeal to the scientific world of that day as well as to politicians and the religious world. I am amazed how even today people are taken in by the phoniest kinds of things. Someone has asked me, "Why do you think that happens?" I believe the answer can be expressed like this, "Those who do not stand for something will fall for anything." People who are not rooted and grounded in the Word of God will fall for all kinds of signs.

"Lying wonders" will produce an effect upon observers. In that day, people all over the world will be talking about the Man of Sin, saying, "My, this world ruler we have is a great fellow. Look at what he can do!"

Who is it that will fall for his lying wonders? Those who would not believe the gospel—

> **And with all deceivableness of unrighteousness in them that perish; because they received not the love of the truth, that they might be saved [2 Thess. 2:10].**

He will do this "with all deceivableness of unrighteousness in them that perish." Why?—"because they received not the love of the truth, that they might be saved." I *do* believe that the gospel is going to go out to the ends of the earth. It may even be the church that accomplishes this. I think it is penetrating pretty well today by radio into areas where individuals cannot go. But there will be those who hear and refuse to receive the truth.

> **And for this cause God shall send them strong delusion, that they should believe a lie [2 Thess. 2:11].**

God will let the world believe a lie. Why does He do that? Isn't that a little unfair? No, it is just like it was when God hardened Pharaoh's heart. Pharaoh wasn't weeping for the children of Israel, longing to let them go free, being held back from his good intentions by God! If you think that, you are entirely wrong. Pharaoh did not want to let them go, and what God did was to force him to make a stand and come to a decision. God forced him into a situation which revealed what was already in his heart. We see a lot of people pussy-footing around today. They won't take a stand for God. They won't listen to the gospel. They are closed to it. God graciously gives them His Word, but they don't want it. After they have heard the Word of God but have refused to accept it, God will send them "strong delusion." Why? Because they would not receive the truth. Then they are open to believe the lie.

People who have stopped going to churches where they heard the gospel are wide open to the cults and the "isms" of our day. That is why so many of the cultists go around on Sunday morning, knocking at doors. They know that the weak people will not be in church on Sunday morning. They are not interested enough in the Word of God to be in church. The cults know that they can get those people, because if they will not receive the truth, they are open for anything else that comes along.

I have been simply amazed at some intelligent people who have sat in church, heard the gospel, rejected it, and then turned to the wildest cult imaginable. They will follow some individual who is absolutely a phony—not giving out the Word of God at all. Why? Because God says that is the way it is: When people reject the truth, they will believe the lie.

God is separating the sheep from the goats. God uses the best way in the world to do it. If people will not receive the love of the truth, then God sends them a "strong delusion, that they should believe a lie." What is the "lie"? The lie of Antichrist is that Jesus Christ is not the Lord, that He is not who He says He is. He will tell people that they are really smart in not becoming religious nuts who believe in Jesus. He'll have some good explanation for the departure of the saints from the earth at the Rapture and will congratulate the people on having waited to build a kingdom on earth with him. The people will believe him and will believe that Antichrist will bring them the Millennium. They will not realize that they are entering into the Great Tribulation. That is the lie, and people will believe it because they believed not the truth.

That they all might be damned who believed not the truth, but had pleasure in unrighteousness [2 Thess. 2:12].

God is going to judge those who have rejected the truth. I have said this many times, and I am going to say it again: If you can sit and read the Word of God in this book and continue to reject Jesus Christ, then you are wide open for anything that comes along to delude and deceive you. You will never be able to go into the presence of God and say, "I never heard the gospel." If you turn your back on the Lord Jesus Christ, then you are wide open for delusion and you are a subject for judgment. As a believer giving out the gospel, I am a savor of life to those that are saved and a savor of death to those that perish (see 2 Cor. 2:15–16). I have really put you out on a limb, because you cannot say you have never heard the gospel. You have heard it, and you have probably heard it in several different places. If you reject Jesus Christ, then I am the savor of death to you. If you accept Jesus Christ as your own Lord and Savior, then I am the savor of life to you.

PRACTICALITY OF CHRIST'S COMING

Now Paul moves into the practical side of this epistle. In the light of the knowledge of future events, the believer should live a life that demonstrates that he believes in the coming of Christ. Believing in the coming of Christ doesn't mean to run out and look up into the sky and say, "Oh, I wish Jesus would come!" That is just pious nonsense. It will be manifest in three different ways if a person believes in the coming of Christ: it will affect his attitude toward the Word, his walk, and his work.

BELIEVERS SHOULD BE ESTABLISHED IN THE WORD

But we are bound to give thanks alway to God for you, brethren beloved of the Lord, because God hath from the beginning chosen you to salvation through sanctification of the Spirit and belief of the truth:

Whereunto he called you by our gospel, to the obtaining of the glory of our Lord Jesus Christ [2 Thess. 2:13–14].

I believe these two verses give the total spectrum of salvation. In other words, they give you salvation "from Dan to Beer-sheba"—all the way from the past, the present, and down into the future.

1. "Chosen you to salvation." This is so clearly taught in Romans 8: "And we know that all things work together for good to them that love God, to them who are the called according to his purpose. [Dr. R. A. Torrey used to say that this verse was a soft pillow for a tired heart. It surely is that.] For whom he did foreknow, he also did predestinate to be conformed to the image of his Son, that he might be the firstborn among many brethren. Moreover whom he did predestinate, them he also called: and whom he called, them he also justified: and whom he justified, them he also glorified. What shall we then say to these things? If God be for us, who can be against us?" (Rom. 8:28-31).

That is exactly what Paul is writing here in 2 Thessalonians: "God hath from the beginning chosen you to salvation." That looks back to the past. All I know is what it says, and I believe it. Do you mean to tell me that God chose us before we even got here? Spurgeon used to put it something like this: "I am glad God chose me before I got here, because if He had waited until I got here He never would have chosen me." It simply means that you do not surprise God when you trust Christ. But there is another side of the coin: "Whosoever will may come." The "whosoever wills" are the chosen ones, and the "whosoever won'ts" are the nonelect. Jesus said, ". . . If any man thirst, let him come unto me, and drink" (John 7:37). That is a legitimate offer of salvation—a sincere, definite offer with no complications attached. If you don't come, the reason is not because you are not elected. Not at all. The reason you don't come is that you're not thirsty; that is, you don't think you need a Savior. If you are thirsty, then come to Christ.

2. "Through sanctification of the Spirit." "Chosen you to salvation" looked back to the past, and now sanctification by the Spirit looks to the present. You are sanctified both as to position and as to practice. When you accept Jesus Christ as your own Savior, you are in Christ—that is positional sanctification; that is the past tense of salva-

tion. Then there is also the practical side of sanctification which concerns your life. Through the Spirit of God you are to grow in grace.

3. "Belief of the truth." That means that a believer is going to study the Word of God. That is the way he is going to grow and develop.

4. "To the obtaining of the glory of our Lord Jesus Christ." This is future. This refers to the Rapture. "Beloved, now are we the sons of God, and it doth not yet appear what we shall be: but we know that, when he shall appear, we shall be like him; for we shall see him as he is" (1 John 3:2). Then there is the statement in Colossians 1:27, "To whom God would make known what is the riches of the glory of this mystery among the Gentiles; which is Christ in you, the hope of glory." That looks forward to the future. What a glorious, wonderful prospect we have before us!

We see that these two verses have given us the full spectrum of salvation: we *have been* saved, we *are being* saved, we *shall be* saved. It is all the work of God.

> **Therefore, brethren, stand fast, and hold the traditions which ye have been taught, whether by word, or our epistle [2 Thess. 2:15].**

Paul is referring to what he had taught them when he was with them. It is the Word which enables the believer to stand and be stable.

> **Now our Lord Jesus Christ himself, and God, even our Father, which hath loved us, and hath given us everlasting consolation and good hope through grace,**

> **Comfort your hearts, and stablish you in every good word and work [2 Thess. 2:16–17].**

The Lord Jesus Christ brings comfort and consolation to our hearts. He does this through His Word. That will establish us in every good word and work. The study of the Word of God will lead to the work of the Lord.

Not only will the Word of God "comfort" us, but it will also edify us. "Stablish you" means we are to be rooted and grounded in the Word of God so that we are not carried away by every wind of doctrine. Our minds and hearts will be centered on Him. That will keep us from going out after every fad of the day and reading every new book that comes off the press. Nor will we be running to little study courses here and there to be built up for the moment. We need to be *established* in the faith.

It is the Word of God then that will lead you to do the work of God. In chapter 3 we will see that believers should also be established in their walk and in their work down here. You see, it is rather deceitful (to yourself and others) to talk about how much you love the coming of the Lord if you do not study His Word. Then your belief does not manifest itself in your life and it doesn't make you work. If you really believe Christ is coming, you're going to be busy working for Him. You are going to give account to Him someday. If He is going to be here tomorrow, we want to be busy today. We shouldn't have our noses pressed against the window looking for Him to come, or to be always looking up into heaven for Him. Instead, we should be looking around doing the work of the Lord down here. That is the greatest proof that we believe in His coming.

CHAPTER 3

THEME: The practicality of Christ's coming

Chapter 2 concluded with the fact that believers should be established in the Word—the Word of God. Paul spoke about God comforting our hearts and establishing us in every good word and work. This has to do with loyalty to the person of the Lord Jesus Christ. Also Paul spoke in chapter 2, verses 13–14, of the marvelous position we have in Christ. We are chosen—"God hath from the beginning chosen you to salvation through sanctification of the Spirit." And we are called of God "to the obtaining of the glory of our Lord Jesus Christ." This is heady stuff! It is exciting and thrilling.

Now here in chapter 3 Paul says that there are certain responsibilities that we have as believers. As Paul put it to the Ephesian believers, ". . . walk worthy of the vocation wherewith ye are called" (Eph. 4:1). Now Paul is saying the same thing to the Thessalonian believers.

BELIEVERS SHOULD BE ESTABLISHED
IN THEIR WALK

Finally, brethren, pray for us, that the word of the Lord may have free course, and be glorified, even as it is with you:

And that we may be delivered from unreasonable and wicked men: for all men have not faith [2 Thess. 3:1–2].

He is saying here that the Word of God enables the believer to walk before the wicked world. The Word establishes a believer in his walk.

"Finally, brethren"—he is coming to the conclusion of his letter.

"Pray for us." Prayer is something that every believer can engage in. I do not think prayer is a gift of the Spirit. Prayer is something that

all believers should do. Every work must have prayer behind it if it is
to succeed. Every successful evangelist and preacher of the Word,
every teacher of the Word who is being used of God, has people who
are praying for him. Paul is asking the Thessalonians for prayer so that
"the word of the Lord may have free course." Paul had a very unique
ministry. He was a missionary. He was an evangelist as we think of
evangelists today. Actually that word *evangelist* in the New Testament
means "missionary." Also, he was a pastor and a teacher of the Word.
He fulfilled all those offices, and he had fulfilled them all to the Thessalonians. He had led them to the Lord and taught them; now he is
acting as their pastor in his letters. He is not only instructing them in
the Word, but he is attempting to comfort them and to counsel them.
One of the things he enjoins them to do is *pray*. "Pray for us, that the
Word of the Lord may have free course, and be glorified, even as it is
with you."

You cannot pray for Paul today, but you can pray for Vernon. I
would appreciate your prayers that the Word of the Lord as I give it out
may have free course and be glorified. The Word of God needs to be
exalted today. Pray that people will exalt the Word of God in their own
lives. It troubles me and it worries me to see that even those who claim
to believe the Word of God give so little attention to it. Pray that if
people profess to believe the Word of God, they will get into it and
find out what it says.

My friend, let me urge you to pray for your pastor. Let me say
something very carefully. I know what it is to be a pastor, and I know
what it is to be a Bible teacher holding conferences. I want to say to
you that it is a lot easier to go around and hold conferences than it is to
be a pastor. A pastor has a great responsibility because, very frankly,
he deals with a great many folk who are unreasonable. Paul asks
prayer that he "may be delivered from unreasonable and wicked
men." Did you know that there are wicked persons in the church? A
pastor needs to be delivered from such folk.

The work of an evangelist is like the work of an obstetrician. He
delivers the little baby into the world, and that is quite an undertak-
ing, of course. But then he turns over the little one to the pediatrician.

He is the one who sees to it that his diet is right, that he is burped properly, that he gets his shots, and so forth. The pastor, you see, is the pediatrician. He is the one who must deal with cantankerous saints and baby Christians. That is quite a job. My heart goes out to the pastor.

When I go out to speak at conferences, I meet some wonderful pastors. The only churches I want to go to are the ones where the pastor is preaching and teaching the Word of God and stands for the things of God. On the other side of the coin, that is the only kind of man who will have me in his pulpit! Recently, as we left such a church, I said to my wife: "We have had a wonderful ministry here at this church for the week. I've been here just long enough—I think these people are wonderful, and they think I am wonderful! I left before they got acquainted with me and I got acquainted with them. Also I think I helped the pastor; he tells me that I did. But he is the one who is carrying the burden and the load there. He is the one who has the problems. I can simply walk away from them." I think the work of an evangelist or of an itinerant Bible teacher, as some of us are, is easy compared to the work of the man who is the pastor.

Paul asked for prayer that he might be delivered from "unreasonable and wicked men." I find that the spreading of the gospel is hindered more by people in the church than by anything else. No liquor industry, no barroom, no gangster ring has ever attacked me—at least I have never known about it. But I have had so-called saints in the churches attack me. As you know, in our churches we have the saints and the "ain'ts," and there are a lot of "ain'ts." They can give a pastor a rough time. It's too bad that we can't all settle down and give out the Word of God.

Now when he says, "For all men have not faith," that is really "the faith." All men do not have the faith. That is, they do not hold to the doctrines as the apostles taught them. The foundation of the church rests upon the doctrine which the apostles have given to the church. That is what we should teach and preach.

It is one thing to hold the truth of the coming of Christ, to love His appearing; but it is another thing to walk worthy of that great truth.

This is what Paul is writing about to the Thessalonians. If we really love His appearing, we will prove it by our relationship to the Word of God and by our walk through this life.

But the Lord is faithful, who shall stablish you, and keep you from evil [2 Thess. 3:3].

That is so wonderful! I have let Him down on several occasions, but He has never let me down. He is faithful. He is always faithful. Christians should hold tenaciously to this little verse. The Lord is faithful, and He will establish you.

Christians need to be established. Right now the home is in disarray, the church is in disarray, and the lives of believers are in disarray. We need to be *established*. How can you as a believer be established? By coming to the Word of God and letting it have its influence in your life. The Lord operates through His Word. The Word of God will keep you from evil. Someone has said, "The Bible will keep you from sin, and sin will keep you from the Bible."

And we have confidence in the Lord touching you, that ye both do and will do the things which we command you [2 Thess. 3:4].

Christians are commanded to do certain things, and there are specific commandments for Christians. We saw that in Paul's first epistle to the Thessalonians where he records twenty-two commandments in the fifth chapter. There are not only ten but twenty-two commandments which the believers are to do. The Lord Jesus said, "If you love Me, keep My commandments" (see John 14:15) and these are His commandments.

Paul had "confidence in the Lord touching" them. He committed them to the Lord with the confidence that they were doing and would continue doing the things which he commanded. He believed that this Thessalonian church which had a wonderful testimony would continue to maintain that testimony.

**And the Lord direct your hearts into the love of God,
and into the patient waiting for Christ [2 Thess. 3:5].**

The believer is to walk in "the love of God." My friend, if you are walking today in the sunshine of His love, the love of God is shed abroad in your heart and you know He loves you. And you can manifest that love by the power of the Spirit, because only the Spirit of God can make God's love real to us. Love is a fruit of the Spirit. You can't naturally love every Tom, Dick, and Harry—and I'm of the opinion God does not expect that of us. Paul wrote to the Philippian Christians that our love is to be in *judgment*, which implies that we should be careful about loving those around us. There are folk who will hurt us if we open our arms to them.

"Into the patient waiting for Christ." This does not mean that you are to argue about being premillennial or pretribulational or posttribulational or amillennial, but that you are to be patiently waiting for the coming of Christ. Oh, what wonderful verses these are!

**Now we command you, brethren, in the name of our
Lord Jesus Christ, that ye withdraw yourselves from
every brother that walketh disorderly, and not after the
tradition which he received of us [2 Thess. 3:6].**

"Now we command you, brethren"—Paul doesn't beat around the bush!

The believer is not to walk with the "disorderly." I know men who insist that we should go into the barrooms, sit down with the drunkard and have a beer with him as we witness to him. Unfortunately, I know of a young lady who became an alcoholic by following that procedure. God says that we are to "withdraw" ourselves from the disorderly. Certainly we are to witness to them, but we are not to fraternize on their level.

God makes it very clear whom we are to follow—

> For yourselves know how ye ought to follow us: for we
> behaved not ourselves disorderly among you [2 Thess.
> 3:7].

Birds of a feather flock together. You will be like the crowd you run
around with. Believers need to be very careful about the company
they keep and the people with whom they associate.

BELIEVERS SHOULD BE ESTABLISHED
IN THEIR WORK

The Thessalonians were walking in a right relationship to the Lord
Jesus, and they were being persecuted for it. Paul comforted them,
instructed, and encouraged them. Now he lets them know that he also
is undergoing persecution and difficulty. And, friend, if you stand for
the Lord, it will cost you something.

We have seen that the believer is to be established in the Word of
God. Then we have noted how important the *walk* of the believer is,
and how his walk should be grounded in the Word. Now we come to
the *work* of the believer, which is also very practical. This involves
things in which we need to be engaged—that the Word of God may
have its way in our hearts and lives.

> Neither did we eat any man's bread for nought; but
> wrought with labour and travail night and day, that we
> might not be chargeable to any of you [2 Thess. 3:8].

"Neither did we eat any man's bread for nought"—that is, for nothing;
he paid for what he ate.

"But wrought with labour and travail night and day, that we might
not be chargeable to any of you." His practice was that he would not let
anyone pay him for his missionary work among them. I think this
applied especially to his first missionary journey. When he arrived in
town as a missionary, there was no reservation for him at the local
motel. There was no stipend given to him, no love offering taken for
him the first time he was there. He was very careful about paying his

own way. He mentions that to the Thessalonians and also to the Corinthians. When he was establishing churches he supported himself by tentmaking.

However, after the churches were established and Paul had come back to visit them a second and a third time, he did receive an offering from them. He makes it clear to the Galatians that they should give. He thanks the Philippians for their gift. He himself took an offering on his third missionary journey to be given to the poor saints in Jerusalem. Obviously, the great truth of the coming of Christ had not caused Paul to become some sort of a fanatic or to take some unreasonable position in relation to money matters.

In every age there are fanatical people. In the last century there were those who expected the return of Christ; so they sold their homes and property, wrapped themselves in white sheets and got on the top of the roof to wait for the Lord to come! There were several actions which identified them as fanatics. For example, why get on the roof? Couldn't the Lord draw a person into the air from the ground as easily as from a roof? If one needed to get up on a roof, then wouldn't a mountaintop be better? And then, why in the world would one need a white sheet? I think the Lord is going to furnish us with suitable coverings when we come into His presence. And why would they sell their property and turn it into money? Did they think they could take the money with them? You see, people can do some very peculiar, senseless things because they say they believe in the soon coming of Christ. The fact is that there is no other doctrine in the Bible that will make you work harder or more sensibly for Christ. If you believe that He is coming, you will work for Him. You will be busy for the Lord in some phase of His work. You will be putting out a few seeds of the Word of God in the field of the world so that they might bring forth a harvest.

**Not because we have not power, but to make ourselves
an ensample unto you to follow us [2 Thess. 3:9].**

Paul is saying that as an apostle who had led them to the Lord and established a church among them, he had the right, the authority, to claim an offering. However, he did not do this because he wanted to be an example to the believers in Thessalonica that they might not be led to some fanatical position.

A young couple who had been in my classes when I taught at a Bible institute were inclined toward fanaticism. They thought they were super-duper saints, way out ahead of everyone else. But their exam papers were graded Cs or Ds, because they didn't really know the Word, although they affected to be very spiritual. (Incidentally, I don't think a person can be truly spiritual and be ignorant of the Word of God.) They came to me after I had become a pastor in that city and said they wanted to go to the mission field. They attended the church I served although they were not members. I asked them if they had their financial support. They said no. I asked, "Do you mean that you are going to the mission field without support?" "Oh," they said, "we're going to trust the Lord." Well, I said, "It's nice to trust the Lord, but can't you trust Him to raise your support here? Must you wait until you get into the mission field to trust Him for support? Why don't you get under a reputable mission board and work with them? If the Lord has called you to go to the mission field, He will raise up support for you—the Lord will lay your needs on the hearts of certain folk who will pray for you and support you financially." No, they didn't want to do it that way, they were just going to trust the Lord. Well, this young couple went out to the mission field, and there they became casualties. They had to be brought home with money that some friends raised to pay their passage. Since that time they have separated and are divorced. She is married again. I have heard that he has lost his faith altogether, although I doubt that he ever really had faith. Their behavior was foolish and fanatical.

Paul was making missionary work very practical. He supported himself by working with his hands, and he did it to be an example to the Thessalonian believers. He is going to make a point of this in the next verse.

For even when we were with you, this we commanded you, that if any would not work, neither should he eat [2 Thess. 3:10].

A believer who is looking for the Lord to return is not a dreamer; he is a worker. No work—no food. That is the rule laid down by the apostle. "If any would not work, neither should he eat."

It is amazing how fanatical people can get about these things. The dean of men at Moody Bible Institute told about an incident that happened about fifty years ago. Two young men roomed together who were other examples of those super-duper saints who thought they were completely sanctified. One day they didn't appear in the dining room for breakfast or for lunch or for dinner; so the dean went up to see what was the problem. They were just sitting there, looking out into space. He asked them if they were sick. No, they weren't sick. "Then why haven't you come down for meals?" They said, "We're just trusting the Lord. We are waiting for Him to tell us whether we should go down to eat." "Are you hungry?" They admitted that they were hungry. "Don't you think that is one of the ways the Lord has of letting you know that you ought to go down to eat?" They said, "No, we are waiting for special revelation from Him, and we are not going to move until then." So the dean said to them, "I have news for you. You *are* going to move, but not down to the dining room. You are going to move out of school. You cannot stay here." There is no place for that kind of fanaticism.

Today we are seeing a kind of fanaticism in the area of prophecy. It is quite interesting that in this epistle which deals largely in prophecy, almost half of it is given over to that which is practical. Paul puts the emphasis on the practical side of the great truth of the coming of Christ for His church. It is one thing to get fanatical about prophecy; it is quite another thing to believe the prophetic truth and then have it meshed and geared into our living down here so that it becomes practical and working.

We are to work while we wait. A gardener for a large estate in northern Italy was conducting a visitor through the castle and the beautiful, well-groomed grounds. As the visitor had lunch with the gardener and his wife, he commended them for the beautiful way they were keeping the gardens. He asked, "By the way, when was the last time the owner was here?" "It was about ten years ago," the gardener said. The visitor asked, "Then why do you keep up the gardens in such an immaculate, lovely manner?" The gardener answered, "Because I'm expecting him to return." He persisted, "Is he coming next week?" The gardener replied, "I don't know when he is coming, but I am expecting him today." Although he didn't come that day, he was living in the light of the owner's imminent return. The gardener wasn't hanging over the gate, watching down the road to see whether his master was coming. He was in the garden, trimming, cutting, mowing, planting. He was busy. That is what Paul is talking about when he says we should be established in the work of the Lord in view of the fact that He is returning.

"If any would not work, neither should he eat." You see, the Thessalonians had a few fanatics who simply withdrew themselves and decided that they were going to spend all their time looking for the Lord's return. Paul writes, "Don't feed them. They have to go to work."

> **For we hear that there are some which walk among you disorderly, working not at all, but are busybodies [2 Thess. 3:11].**

Here we are told the situation. There were some who were not working at anything constructive. They were not interested in getting out the Word of God, but they were busy—they were busybodies. They were really making a nuisance of themselves, and they were causing trouble in the church in Thessalonica. It takes just one bad apple to spoil the barrel; it takes just one little fly to spoil the ointment; and one fanatic in the church can affect the spiritual life of a great many people. That is the reason Paul had said before that they were to withdraw themselves from the ones who walk disorderly, and I'm sure he had the busybodies in mind. They were busy as termites and just as effective as termites in the church at Thessalonica.

> **Now them that are such we command and exhort by our Lord Jesus Christ, that with quietness they work, and eat their own bread [2 Thess. 3:12].**

This doesn't sound very spiritual, does it? It doesn't sound very theological. But it certainly is practical. It would solve a great many problems in the average church if the busybodies, the troublemakers, would work with quietness and do something constructive. It is interesting that the man who was the biggest troublemaker in any church that I served was the smallest contributor—and I found that out by accident. The treasurer of the church was talking to me about the trouble this fellow had been, and I said, "Well, he is a man of means, and I suppose a very generous giver, and he naturally is interested in how his money is being spent." The treasurer looked at me and laughed. He said, "That man gives ten dollars a year for the Lord's work!" Believe me, he certainly gave us more than ten dollars worth of trouble! There must have been people like that in Thessalonica. Paul says that they were to quietly go to work and mind their own business.

But ye, brethren, be not weary in well-doing [2 Thess. 3:13].

How wonderful this is! A believer who holds the blessed hope should not grow weary of working for the Lord. As Moody put it, "I get weary in the work, but not weary of the work."

And if any man obey not our word by this epistle, note that man, and have no company with him, that he may be ashamed [2 Thess. 3:14].

People in the church ought to withdraw from troublemakers in the church. However, many people more or less court their favor, because they don't want those people to talk about them, knowing they have vicious tongues. But withdrawing from the gossips would be the best thing that could happen in many churches.

Yet count him not as an enemy, but admonish him as a brother [2 Thess. 3:15].

An attempt should be made to win the wayward member.

> **Now the Lord of peace himself give you peace always by all means. The Lord be with you all [2 Thess. 3:16].**

Isn't this lovely!

> **The salutation of Paul with mine own hand, which is the token in every epistle: so I write [2 Thess. 3:17].**

This is an epistle from Paul signed with his own hand.

> **The grace of our Lord Jesus Christ be with you all. Amen [2 Thess. 3:18].**

His letter ends with a benediction. It is the conclusion of a wonderful epistle which teaches that the knowledge of prophecy, rather than leading to fanaticism or laziness, brings peace to the heart.

BIBLIOGRAPHY

(Recommended for Further Study)

Hiebert, D. Edmond. *The Thessalonian Epistles, A Call to Readiness.* Chicago, Illinois: Moody Press, 1971. (An excellent, comprehensive treatment.)

Hogg, C. F. and Vine, W. E. *The Epistles of Paul to the Thessalonians.* Grand Rapids, Michigan: Kregel Publications, 1914. (An excellent, comprehensive treatment.)

Ironside, H. A. *Addresses of I and II Thessalonians.* Neptune, New Jersey: Loizeaux Brothers, n.d.

Kelly, William. *The Epistles to the Thessalonians.* Oak Park, Illinois: Bible Truth Publishers, 1893.

MacDonald, William. *Letters to the Thessalonians.* Kansas City, Missouri: Walterick Publishers, 1969.

Ryrie, Charles C. *First and Second Thessalonians.* Chicago, Illinois: Moody Press, 1959. (Fine, inexpensive survey.)

Walvoord, John F. *The Thessalonian Epistles.* Grand Rapids, Michigan: Zondervan Publishing House, 1955.